The Opposite of Noise

The Power Of Competitive Intelligence

BENJAMIN GILAD, PH.D
CEO, ACADEMY OF COMPETITE INTELLIGENCE
www.academyci.com, www.giladwargames.com

ben@giladwargames.com

"Engaging and entertaining. There is no other competitive intelligence training/workshops that compare"

- HERE Technology

"If you are not using the information in this course, your competition is! Very thorough, relevant, and valuable lessons that can be immediately applied to your Competitive Intelligence regime. Highly recommend"

- Kevin Crouch, SAIC (Cross-Competitor Analysis)

"Great Program, highly recommended to anyone doing strategy or competitive intelligence work!"

- Vlad Zaitsev, Dir. Strategic Insights & Analytics, Abbott

"ACI is a pioneer in advancing Next-Gen Intel. Content substance - directly applicable to your next decision at work leading to career satisfaction and advancement (Pertinent)"

- Elizabeth Lamoreaux, Collins Aerospace

"CI is NOT Market Research. Period. ACI teaches you to be a strategic thinker."

- Vivian Ho, Strategy & Operations, Elanco

"This training was by far the most engaging and interactive virtual courses I've attended."

- Christopher Hauke, Schott AG

"I got new insights on all levels... I will also work a lot harder to make sure not to just send information upwards but only develop and track CI information that will be used for real. I'm in an internal CI workshop this week and are seeing things with new eyes."

- Bjorn Kopniwski, Ericsson

"Whether it's a new analyst on your CI team taking the basic courses or an established practitioner coming back for advanced training this is the best CI training available. Competitive Intelligence training through ACI is not your ordinary training program."

**- Stacy Keding, Director,
Strategic Competitive Intelligence Eli Lilly and Co.**

"ACI was one of the best training sessions I have ever attended"

- Amy Blaha

"High impact. High value. I am very happy with the extremely useful tools, methods and techniques"

- Luciano Oviedo, Intel

"There is no better way to learn your industry than through this course – especially your own company's blindspots! Fabulous.

- Tyler Oborn, Mars

"This course was above and beyond my expectations providing the right mix between theory, practice and networking. Very empowering"

- Hanadi Said, TEVA Pharmaceuticals

"I've gained a different and invaluable perspective on the impact I can make on strategic decisions – I'm more motivated to "preach" the CI culture at my own company"

- Eden Wells, Novartis

"Ben Gilad will take you on a journey that will be an eye-opener in how strategic your company is and give you tools to question status-quo"

- Florence Theys, SCA

"It challenged my sense of understanding and moved me to a new dimension in strategy"

- Hauwa Ali – Nigerian National Petroleum Corp.

"An outstanding resource for viewing your industry and competitors in a way that can potentially move the needle"

- Kevin Doll, Re/Max

"Great course to stretch your brain and add to how you think about the market, every market"

- Catherine Costa, Allscripts

"If you want to improve your CI skills, this is the course you should take"

- Eduardo Quintero, Janssen

"If you can only take one course, make it this one!"

- Brad Puckett, Little Caesars Enterprises Inc.

"This course should be required of anyone planning to establish a new CI function in a company"

- David Owen, Nuance Communications

"The honest dialogue about corporate America & how strategy works in it, will help anyone in their own organization. It is easy to see how ACI has become a cornerstone for CI".

- Jeff Orf, The Boeing Co.

"The best training course I have taken in a dozen years with direct, immediate applicability to our way of thinking"

- Dave Dusza, Northrop Grumman

"An incredible set of pivotal lessons on CI. This is an absolute must have for everyone in the CI profession"

- Carlos Cruz, Chevron Phillips Chemicals

"Fantastic course on tools that help create and enhance a business intelligence acumen"

- Matthew Chandler, ExxonMobil

"The combination of theory, practice and world class teachers makes this one of the most valuable five days of my career"

- Hanadi Said, TEVA Pharmaceuticals

"You will distinctly remember Ben's course so much more than any other course you have taken before. His energy, wisdom and experience in strategic intelligence is unparalleled. Undoubtedly the best CI master in the world...and also the funniest"

- Heresh Rezavandi, UCB

"Refreshing, Challenging, and Life Changing"

- Maggie Hill, Berry Plastics

"Outstanding content, engaging presentations which are all grounded in practical experience"

- Stuart deGeus, Little Caesar Enterprises

"Discovering all the activities that have nothing to do with strategy was eye-opening"

- Steven Ramirez, Symantec

"Ben takes you out of your comfort zone in order to help you develop…"

- Gerald Flynn, Amica

"If you are interested in winning in the market place, you must attend this course"

- Robert Cornell, Lexmark International

"I have been so impressed with the content and quality of instructors. Top notch – best ever!"

- Jennifer Isbister, EnCana

"It was like a great movie that I didn't want to take a bio break for"

- Lynda Dube, Unum

"Makes you feel the passion for CI art"

- Daniel Benmuhar, Cemex

"It changes the way I see the company environment"

- Daniel Benmuhar, Cemex

"Great education on how to view & analyze the industries"

- Naren Patel, GlaxoSmithKline

"Amazingly insightful, changed the way I look at data and information"

- **Mohamed Kesseba, Emirates Integrated Telecommunications Group**

"Excellent interactive course – highly recommend to all companies with any interest in CI"

- **James Walsh, Enterprise Ireland**

"I liked it so much I took it twice"

- **Luis Madureira, SCC-Sociedade Central de Cervejas – Heineken**

"This was the most complete CI course I have had. I learned a lot, and there is a lot to think through and more to learn with the items presented. Well worth my long travel and cost. Thank you."

- **Miho Nam, Schweitzer Engineering Laboratories**

"Best training course I have ever attended"

- **Miho Nam, Schweitzer Engineering Laboratories**

"Even when I sat through endless fantastic sessions at a top MBA School with Strategy experts, they still lacked the insightful, realistic, practical approach you showed us in just 2 days. I'm a fan."

- **Blanca Rosales, Novartis**

"My boss in Zürich told me: "you will learn more in 2 weeks in Boston than in all your university time" I know only now he was right."

- **Marco Scafi, ABB Asea Brown Boveri Ltd**

"It's amazing what caliber of people the Academy attracts"

**- Anna Levit, Ortho-McNeil Janssen
Pharmaceuticals, J&J**

"Eye opener, energizing, practical"

- Labouret Gilles, SKF

"Learn CI at ACI is amazing because it is so practical. It's different from just having a theoretical class"

- Renata Teixeira, Petrobras

"I have never visited something so dense, informative and challenging"

- Marc Stoeber, Bayer Animal Health

"Ben Gilad helped me to really strip away the politics and other noise from the corporate environment to focus purely on strategy. A must-have skill to be effective in any business context large or small"

- Lee Razo, Independent Consultant

"The course left me wanting more. I couldn't wait to get back to work to put what I had learned to use.

- Tyler Oborn, Mars

"Revolutionary. Quotes from the teacher that you will often repeat with others"

-Anna Capraro, TetraPak

"The course added value to an analyst's skill set that otherwise would be difficult to learn"

- Sam Patel, ETS

"Unbelievably informative!"

- Jim George, Springboard West Innovations

The Opposite of Noise
Copyright © 2021 by Benjamin Gilad, Ph.D

Book Cover designed by Trisha Fuentes

ISBN: 979-8481879833 (Paperback)

*To my wife, Shirly, the partner to our "empty nest."
With you in it, it is never empty.*

*And to my children, Corinne and Milo: You might have flown the nest, but
you are always on my mind.*

Acknowledgments

To the loyal readers of my The Skeptical Analyst column, who offered some great alternative titles such as

SHUT UP- no, not *you*: How to shut out the noise and move up the competitive food chain (Stepanie Grey)

How to be Competitively Savvy: Intelligence that drives smart business decisions (Hanna Haris)

Hustling for Opportunities - Good decision making in an uncertain world (Babette BenSoussan)

Breaking Away from the Pack: Making Competitive Intelligence the Growth Engine of Your Company (Enrico Vonghia)

And a few variations on **Haystack** and **needles**.

And my absolute non sequitur, **Damn, I was on vacation!** (Quentin Smith). Think about this for a minute. In this fast changing world, it's such a great metaphor.

All more than suitable. I had a hard choice. But all choices are tricky as they stand for what you say No to, not just to what you say Yes.

Contents

Chapter 1:
The Lost "Voice of the Market"

There are many definitions for the term "competitive intelligence." Some define it as legally obtained information about competitors (which is a *part* of it), while others believe it's the search for competitors' secrets (which is *not at all* a part of it).

Some say it should solely support salespeople (no, it shouldn't), some prescribe it as crucial for top management (it is), and there are even those believing it should keep board members tuned to the reality of the market (a very lofty goal). In this book, I define competitive intelligence (CI) as strategic market insight: A *new angle* on the competitive reality pointing to an opportunity to gain an edge over other players in a market. When we define intelligence as insight rather than mere information, it is clear top executives do not receive all the competitive intelligence they need to make strategic decisions.

They just don't know what to do about it.

I've been diagnosing companies' competitive "blinders" for close to 30 years, ever since I published my book, *Business Blindspots*, in 1994. During "war games" with the world-leading corporations, I go into a room (real or virtual) and listen to teams of managers and executives "role play" competitors. Regardless of which industry a company competes in, there are always discrepancies between top management's beliefs about the competitive reality and field people's observations. The divergence can be critical in the **perception of strategic opportunities** or what many call **market insights.** It often looks like the two levels- top executives versus managers and analysts- live in different realities.

In discussing the discrepancies with management, one frequent claim is "they just don't see what we see from here." This claim is valid: The two sides are exposed to different sources and different levels of information. What management often doesn't realize, though, is that the reverse is also true.

Another claim is that less senior managers and analysts just "don't have all the data." What it means is not that middle management, salespeople, and professional analysts do not have *enough* information, but they do not have the *right* kind of information. This claim is also reasonable. The top-level reckons with more factors than their employees. The difference comes down to Big Picture versus local conditions.

The questions companies should always pose are these:

1. Are executives always right and the ranks consistently wrong when perspectives diverge?
2. Can middle managers be taught how to see the Big Picture?
3. Can their market insights be harnessed to help top management change its view?

This last point is crucial for companies' growth.

Every business competes, even Google, even your local church. But one can't compete blindfolded. The bloodline of competing, defined as creating or sustaining a competitive edge, is market insight. Decision-makers discover market insight through the information available to them at the time they make a decision. This information emerges from two primary sources: a decision maker's internal channels and their external contacts. The former includes the layers of employees and executives the decision-maker interacts with, directly or indirectly. The latter consists of consultants, investment bankers, some customers (typically the large ones), peers in leadership positions, research companies, and many other external sources.

When the two streams of information diverge, the decision-makers have a tough call: Should they trust the internal insights or the external ones?

Many management gurus believe companies need external perspectives. This book, however, advances the counter-intuitive idea that decision-makers pay closer attention to the insights of their employees, especially market-facing managers and professionals. The reason is *not* that external sources are unreliable. They are simply never as closely tied with the company's strategy and its implementation, the company's true capabilities, as well as its blinders as the company's market-facing managers. The failure of a plan to capitalize on early opportunities, for one, is often the result of failure to recognize relatively early signals of changing dynamics in a market. Field employees and market-facing managers are quicker to pick up on these than outside advisors, but

no one is listening.

Identifying early change signals is not easy without understanding the source of the change and how it gives rise to strategic opportunities (and risks). The so-called market *insight* is, *by definition,* not apparent to everyone. The Big Picture executives speak about should not be confused with market research or consumer insights. Big picture (market) insight is way broader and more strategic.

If we call early signs of strategic market change, somewhat poetically, the "voice of the market," the first to note those are managers and employees in the various "sensory" functions. Managers in sales, marketing, business development, product management, and technology scouting functions, as well as trained competitive intelligence practitioners, are at the forefront of market change signals. Line managers' perspectives are the "canary in the coal mine" about changes in the competitive landscape. Lacking an effective process to bring these perspectives into management's focus and the hands of top strategy designers, however, forces top executives to rely on the views of outsiders who are always one step behind these changes.

Recognizing the change in market dynamics is at the core of so-called competitive intelligence. However, this insight into the nature and future of competing is just a tiny portion of the information bombarding managers and executives. Options to exploit a changing market dynamic are known as strategic options, and they must follow the insight to gain a competitive edge. Change the term "intelligence" into the less misunderstood "insight," and you get the actual value of competitive intelligence (competitive or strategic insight).

As noted, the information used to identify an opportunity for a competitive edge is not the same as what's available. It's a tiny portion of the bombardment. Thus, formally speaking, I term CI Quotient the ratio of information used in developing insight to the complete information available:

$$\text{CI Quotient: } \frac{\textit{useful information}}{\textit{available information}}$$

The upper limit is 1.0 as it is impossible to use more than what's available to the decision-maker at any moment in time. The lower limit is somewhere in the vicinity of 0.01 as it is not likely that nothing in the information available to decision-makers is helpful as a signal of future events.

Given the inhuman amount of information vying for decision makers' attention, the role of employees in uncovering market insights is becoming critical. How they can do it effectively and how companies can tap into that is the subject of this book. In terms of the simple index above, systematically tapping into employees' insights raises the numerator of useful information.

Without an effective approach to tapping employees, the denominator (available information) increases exponentially, reflecting the growing ease of access to data. As a result, the signal-to-noise ratio (CI quotient) falls below the capacity of management to control. Noise then masks the identification of opportunities and risks, and the result is a competitive surprise followed by competitive failure followed by management shakeup.

Market insight is not synonymous with market research

Opportunities focus on creating and then exploiting competitive edge. Embedded in this edge are *speculations* about the response of third parties to the company's choice of which option to pursue. Unfortunately, third parties' actions/reactions – be they customers, distributors, suppliers, regulators, or competitors - are never known in certainty. While the amount of information available through market research, focus groups, big data analytics of customers' transactions, trade shows, and industry publications is useful to predict *some* of those third parties' reactions, the usefulness decreases the more strategic the company's move is. A move that creates a more significant change in the dynamics between the company and other market players and a bigger deviation from the status quo are complicating factors. For example, would people have predicted the rapid acceptance of Uber or the incredible popularity of Massive Open Online Courses (MOOC) just a decade ago?

With the decrease in the usefulness of available information for strategic decisions affecting a company's performance years into the future comes a simple but powerful implication: Competing and a competitive edge doesn't require more and more data. A/I doesn't give companies the competitive edge. Competitive intelligence does.

It is easier to see the truth in this simple observation by studying how decision-makers spend their time on the job. The overwhelming portion of a day is dedicated to processing and reporting information needed to maintain current operations. Some estimates put this at 73% of managerial time[1]. Thus, a lot of information is processed, but none is about opportunities involving an innovative new advantage.

Some managers believe real-time data provide a competitive edge. In one survey, however, only 19% of executives claimed real-time data improved their company's competitiveness[2]. Real-time data can help companies improve product or service customization by tapping rapidly into customer feedback, but strategic shifts do not require real-time data.

The reverse is also not true: waiting for Big Data, which analyzes thousands or millions of past transactions with customers, or scanning social media discourse risks missing the window for strategic opportunities. Instead, impact on strategy and competitive edge comes from the unique quality of competitive intelligence- market insight based on early signals of opportunities before they are obvious to other players. In other words, neither real-time nor rear-view mirror is what's missing in companies' search for competitiveness. Instead, speculative insight into the future is the key.

Competitive intelligence is misunderstood by many to mean detailed information about competitors, but information is not intelligence, and competitors are not all the high impact players affecting a company's bottom line.

The difference is not just "academic." It's Day and Night. However, it is challenging to recognize competitive intelligence (strategic market insight) in the incredible data noise. Data vendors, A/I sellers, platform developers, and software giants spend significant resources convincing scared corporate executives to buy their panacea to uncertainty in the noise. Yet, at the same time, the reality is all the insights needed to leap the competition are literally under management's nose.

For companies to benefit from employees' market insights, these employees need a simple tool for their search, and their companies need a better model to link their insights to strategic decisions. Section One of this book describes such a tool. Section Two refines the search with "tricks" and tips from hundreds of competition professionals. For management to benefit from employees' perspectives, though, companies need a much more effective competitive intelligence model than what's typical today. Section Three presents a new approach to organizing the hunt for market insight to benefit companies in every industry and all markets.

Tidying up terms and clearing confusion

Busy managers and executives don't bother with dictionary definitions of terms, and for a good reason: precise definitions don't make much of a difference. Common usage trumps precision.

Until it doesn't.

That happens when different interpretations of a term lead to very different behaviors. It's time to de-clutter the house.

Competitive

Colloquially used to describe "on par" with competitors. In Defense and Aerospace industry, when referring to rival bids on multibillion government contracts, "very competitive" stands for "as good as our proposal but cheaper."

To avoid confusing "competitive" with merely lower prices, this book will use competitive edge to refer to a move that will put the company ahead of the rivals, not just "on par" with them.

Strategy

A set of activities aimed at creating a competitive edge by providing unique value to customers.

Competitive strategy

A strategy that reckons with the existence of rivals who naturally have little reason to applaud it. Some critics of the term (associated with Harvard Business School's Professor Michael Porter) suggest it focuses too much on competitors, but these critiques are misplaced. Porter's theory is correct in claiming the success of any strategy depends on others *as well as* the strategist.

Competitive intelligence

A small portion of market information and data that companies use to arrive at strategic market insight.

Market insight

A *previously unknown* perspective on the market uncovering opportunities for a competitive edge while simultaneously considering other players' reactions.

Competitive intelligence quest

The non-deliberate search by managers and executives for market insight (defined above).

Alertness to opportunities

The underlying, subconscious condition fueling the competitive intelligence quest (see Chapter 4).

Information practitioners

All vendors and internal functions collecting, archiving, and routinely distributing all sorts of market data and information (mislabeled "competitive intelligence"). These professionals and agencies have their role in keeping companies informed, but they *do not* provide true market insight since information is not intelligence.

Quick takeaways for the road:

> *Throughtout this book "competitve intelligence" and strategic "market insight" will be used interchangeably. At the end, they amount to pursuing opportunities for edge over other players.*

> *Top management believes lower echelons just don't see what it sees from where it sits. The problem is: it also works in reverse.*

> *One common mistake is to assume that market research/consumer insights are the same as market insight. They are not. As will be shown below, competitve intelligence, or completitive insight, or market insight (terms are used interchangeably) are way broader and more strategic.*

> *Competitive intelligence is always a **tiny portion** of information bombarding management. It's the diamond in the rough, pointing to competitive edge. It is always an insight, never just the information.*

> *Competing doesn't require more and more information. It does require competitive intelligence - the small part of the information available pointing to changes in market dynamics and opening options for pursuing opportunities to reach a new competitive edge.*

Big data, by definition, are always late.

Information is not intelligence and competitors are not all the high impact players affecting a company's bottom line. At times, they are not even the most important.

Chapter 2:
How Do Companies Hunt for Opportunities?

Scenario 1: You are sitting in your (home) office, reading 125 emails, four market reports, and endless other documents you need (or not) to do your job. At the same time, your company is looking for opportunities to grow revenues and profit. Is there anything in the enormous amount of data you process each day that can help your company *beyond* just keeping its current operations running smoothly?

Maybe.

There is just one problem: out of the hundreds of thousands of bits you process daily, the endless meetings you sit through (physically or via Zoom), the barrage of communication addressed to you, or someone else but you are on the distribution list, only a tiny fraction is about possible new opportunities for your company to create an edge.

Do you know which? And as important:

How do you know what is relevant to your management?

Most of us don't. Instead, we read something, we hear something, and we think: That may be useful. We might report it, or not, depending on our experience with such communications, and then, when we hear nothing back, we stop.

Companies do not train their managers to look for market insight. Managers need a simple framework to help them judge what insight is given the company's strategy and capabilities and given its dependence on others' responses for its success. Even if individually they only see a partial picture, collectively, junior and middle managers' "antennas" can transmit market insight no one else can.

If only anyone asked.

Imagine how strong an organization can become if managers collectively looked for opportunities for growth and their perspectives *moved the needle* on the thinking at the top.

The Noise Age

We dub our century the Information Age. This is misleading. It is the noise age. The tiny portion of the information that leads to market insight hides under a pile of data. Do you know how to filter what is mere noise and what can genuinely affect your company's future? A/I and ML (machine learning) don't know unless you tell them (program the algorithm). But if you don't know, how can you create an algorithm?

Companies don't train managers to recognize intelligence as in strategic market insight. So, their search is at best ineffective.

Research shows people, especially younger ones who are used to multiple sources of information on their devices, have a shorter and shorter attention span and still want more information. Yet the fact that more information piles up and gets circulated doesn't mean managers can more easily recognize opportunities. So what do companies do with all that information? Mostly nothing. The table below shows what experts in identifying competitive intelligence say: Only 26% of them regarded insufficient information as an issue for their companies.

Do you agree with this statement: My company has more information and data than it needs to make good decisions		
Answer Options	Response Percent	Response Count
Completely agree	12.9%	27
Agree	35.7%	75
Neutral	25.7%	54
Disagree	22.9%	48
Completely disagree	2.9%	6
answered question		210
skipped question		26

Table 1: Noise level as judged by competitive intelligence managers (n=210, survey date: 2015, Academy of Competitive Intelligence).

How your company competes

Scenario 2: You are a hardworking, dedicated professional. You do your job; you mind your own business; you don't go looking for confrontation or trouble. Your immediate peers respect you. Your boss values you. You don't slack- you are on Slack. And then the company is being hammered in the market, a giant conglomerate swallows it, or worse: It is absorbed by a Private Equity fund because its performance is unsatisfactory. And you are laid off. Why you? You didn't do anything wrong. You didn't make outrageous mistakes. You followed the company's leaders. They fought the battle gallantly, raising the goals, stretching the objectives, motivating you with inspirational speakers. But, alas, the company seemed to have fought yesterday's battle, and the frontline already moved. Is it your fault the company faltered?

Maybe not, but management is often insular. It designs a strategy that can't be implemented successfully because other players in the market – competitors, customers, regulators, suppliers, distributors, disruptors- refuse to play its idea of the game, making the strategy unimplementable.

The following quote from one Benoit Claveranne, Group Chief Transformation Officer, AXA, an insurance giant, sums it up: "One risk we all have is that, at some point, you forget about reality and the market. You think just about your plan, and you start living in your new reality."

Companies are always at risk of losing touch with their markets. Sales managers in the field and professionals in marketing, business development, and brand/product management sense changes in market dynamics long before top management get the memo. But they are not in the loop. A unit President with 10,000 employees can't communicate with each one of them. And managers can't communicate with the chief; they must go through channels. Unfortunately, channels are slow, siloed, and political.

A 2017 survey of 500 senior executives of large companies by the Economist Intelligence Unit and PMI[3] revealed that companies achieving their strategic objectives (named "Leaders") are set apart from those who failed by getting useful information in the right hands at the right time. In the survey, only 10% of the companies did that well. 90% didn't.

The fundamental difference between noise and intelligence

This book touches on the two most essential elements in how companies compete: intelligence and strategy. Intelligence identifies options for strategy; strategy directs the intelligence quest. The symbiotic relationship between intelligence and strategy is intuitively understood. However, the difference between big, small, and medium-sized data and the golden nugget called competitive or strategic insight that affects strategy is often not well understood.

Every company and every manager facing the market collects data. Managers process data into information by employing an intuitive validation process; for example, relying on some sources and not others; Looking at what others use as reliable sources; following some brands of information vendors (Gartner, Forester, WSJ). This process is based on experience, reputation, and other signals of credibility. It's not failproof, but it is good enough.

The problem arises when information –relatively reliable data- remains largely about operations. No one turns it into intelligence - insight about opportunities for a new competitive edge. The overwhelming amount of routine reporting of market news and "competitive developments" is merely competitive information. Since it is not an insight (something new), it is not intelligence.

The Golden Rule of Intelligence: Intelligence is insight, not facts or data.

Corollary 1: Competitive intelligence is valuable information for identifying opportunities (and risks) for a competitive edge. Information that is not used that way is not competitive intelligence, no matter how reliable and trustworthy it is. Usage implies an impact on management perspective.

Figure 1 below visualizes the concept of intelligence. Only one marble is intelligence: The left one. The reason is that it will cause all other marbles to change position.

It has an impact.

If we "measure" intelligence by its impact on management perspective regarding market dynamics, then this "update" of management perspective is the only ROI to be expected of competitive intelligence. Information that doesn't change perspective is useful in routine operational decisions, but only competitive intelligence – market insight - has a critical role in charting and implementing strategy.

The impact can be
- Subtle or substantial
- Quick or delayed
- Recognized and admitted or subconscious and underappreciated
- It operates first and foremost at the cognitive schema level

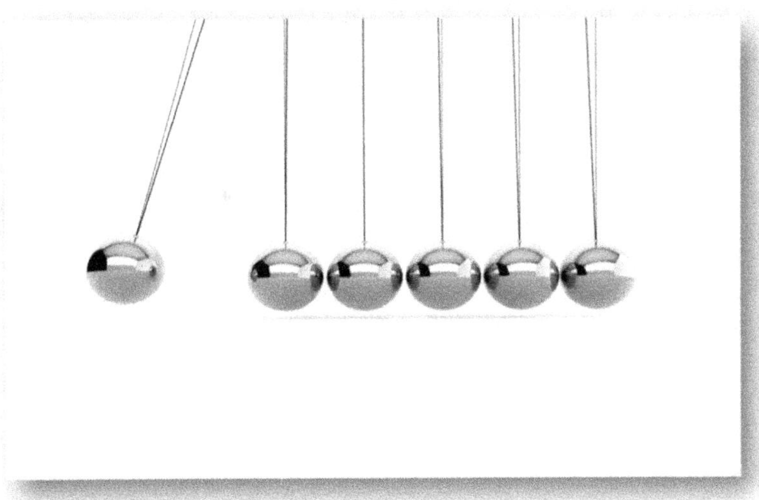

Figure 1 Intelligence visualized

The last point is the most important. Intelligence doesn't necessarily lead to immediate action. It may not be traceable by the user to the moment it had an impact. That's why it is futile to try and quantify intelligence ROI (though there will always be vendors trying to do that). The impact, however, is always on the user's thinking about competition and opportunities for an edge.

Corollary 2: Useful information is not synonymous with "actionable" information; It is not equivalent to "truth"; What is useful is always subjective.

Winners in the competitive arena outthink their opponents. Not outsmart them- that term assumes the other players are dumb. Outthink means being a step ahead in your head at that moment. For some top management teams, it comes down to a Eureka moment based on one significant insight; for others, it is a gradual change in their perspective over time, based on accumulated input from their market-facing managers. The French philosopher Rene Descartes famously said: I think, therefore I am. Let me rephrase it:

I think, therefore, I am competing.

The intelligence process inside a company is a journey. Regardless of the formal format of that process, the significant element is how competitive intelligence changes the way top management thinks about competitive edge before it affects the way it acts (or chooses not to).

Corollary 3: Consensus by experts is meaningless for intelligence because experts typically see opportunities in retrospect.

At times, intelligence (market insight) changes one assumption, and it's enough to have an enormous impact.

Case in Point

In the 70s, commercial aircraft engine company Pratt & Whitney was the leading aircraft engine manufacturer. The DC line of aircraft used its engines. Then over time, competitors - GE and Rolls Royce overtaken P&W. Their engines were the default choice byu Boeing and Airbus on their wide-body aircraft. This relegated P&W to servicig engines on older planes. These were hard times for the venerable company. In the 2000s, the company developed a revolutionary engine based on geared turbofan technology (GTF). It was greener and quieter than competitors' engines.

The problem was the new technology was met with widespread skepticism by authorizative and respectable experts and observers did not view turbofan as a viable alternative to the big jet engines. In a strategy workshop I led for P&W, reams of data and information were available to suggest that P&W's new engine will be a marginal success at best. Conventional wisdom in the industry at the time was that P&W was a "has been". GTF was derided as old technology. Rumors even floated that its parent, United Technologies was considering selling it.

A few single "nuggets" proved crucial in giving rise to market insight out of the pile of information. Surprisingly, the nuggets were negative data. First, it was clear from the information that P&W had no chance of selling the new engine to Boeing because the interlocking boards of Boeing and GE (Boeing CEO at that time came from GE) favored a close relationship with GE. Another reality check and as easily buried nugget was that P&W had no chance of selling the new engine to Airbus because EU's politics favored Rolls Royce, a co-venture of several European countries. None of these nuggets was a big secret and yet none featured prominently with the industry sources. Instead, analysts looked at technical detals, compared performance data, and produced a lot of noise in general.

How did these nuggets become intelligence? P&W's management used them to change its thinking about potential customers for the engine. Instead of wasting time and significant resources competing for Boeing and Airbus' contracts, middle managers in the war game suggested P&W turn to Bombardier (at the time an independent Canadian manufacturer of narrow-body aircraft). The rest has been a miraculous turnaround of the company.[4]

They say opportunity knocks only once. I don't believe this is true but what is true is that intelligence – market insight about an opportunity- knocks quietly. Companies looking to grow need to facilitate this "knock" using the tools in chapters 3 and 4 and the structural model presented later.

Quick takeaways for the road:

Imagine how strong an organization can become if managers collectively looked for opportunities for growth and their perspective moved the needle on the thinking at the top.

Only a miniscule fraction of the information you "process" in any given day is about new opportunities.

Successful strategies rely on getting useful information (i.e., competitive intelligence) into the right hands at the right time. Only 10% of companies know how to do that. The rest are stumbling in the dark.

"One risk we all have is that, at some point, you forget about reality and the market. You think just about your own plan, and you start living in your new reality."

Benoit Claveranne, Group Chief Transformation Officer, AXA

The Golden Rule of Intelligence: Intelligence is insight, not facts or data.

Chapter 3:
A Framework for the Competitive Intelligence Quest

To harness its people's insights about creating a competitive edge, a company should educate employees – especially market-facing managers, salespeople, and professionals- in understanding and assessing the Big Picture. All market insights arise from changes in the Big Picture. Without a high level of understanding of the Big Picture, there is a low probability that insights from the field be strategic enough to survive scrutiny at the top. Moreover, the idea of "crowdsourcing," popular in financing new ventures and as well as in developing Communities of Practice, applies here. "Crowd sourcing" among several large companies suggests that the collective wisdom of a diverse group of managers might be superior in seeing a change in market dynamics that is hidden from an individual manager. For that, however, **a shared platform**- a Big Picture framework – is necessary.

The importance of a shared platform to foster the search for market insights is emphasized by Stan Sthanunathan of Unilever[5]: "The watershed moments.. don't happen by default. They happen by the right people who have a very clear roadmap for making that happen. And the road map for that all starts with...the endpoint of growth in mind."

The roadmap to growth starts with understanding changes in market forces because all growth opportunities emerge from these changes. There are numerous frameworks for analyzing markets and industries. However, most competitive intelligence professionals (CIP™) use the simple yet powerful industry structural model by Michael Porter[6].

Michael Porter created the framework in the late 1970s. While Porter, a Harvard Business School professor of strategy, has been most prominent for his work on generic strategies, his real contribution has been his *evolutionary* perspective on industries and how they change over time.

Porter's most important insight was to explicitly reckon with the role of *multiple* players in the success (and failure) of any strategy.

It is common sense that success is never under a company's total control. This sense is not that common though among executives, especially in successful, dominant firms. They are especially vulnerable, according to research, to the fallacy of over-optimistic assumptions about their ability to control other players' actions and reactions. And then they are surprised, and some pay with their jobs and their employees pay with theirs.

What other players affect a company's success? Here is a partial list.

Category of other market players	Example of action affecting your company
Competitors	Change in strategy
New entrants into your market	Lower price, broader portfolio
Suppliers	Disrupted supply chain
Buyers/customers	Changing preferences and priorities
Substitute offering	"Disruptors" at a lower cost or very different performance than your industry
Regulators	Unintended consequences of new regulation
Partners/ecosystem	Different priorities
Distributors	Adding competing products

Table 2: Market players affecting your company's performance

Figure 2 below is adapted from the top executives' survey by the Economist and PMI cited earlier. The correspondence with Table 2 above is not coincidental. As mentioned earlier, top management tends to have a broader view of the big picture than others in the organization.

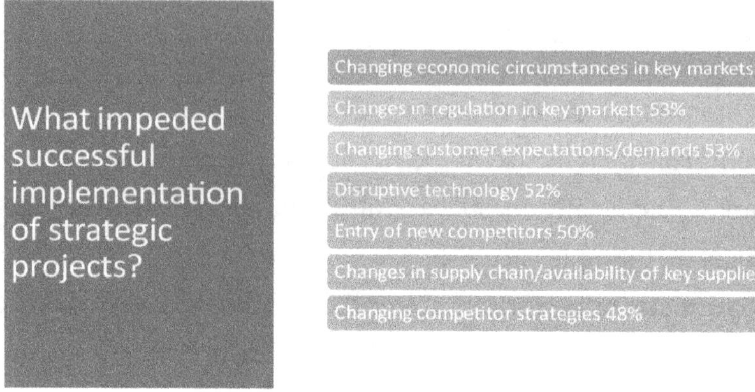

*Figure 2: Factors in strategic **failures***

What was surprising in the Economist/PMI's survey, however, was the findings that companies already track their competitive environment:

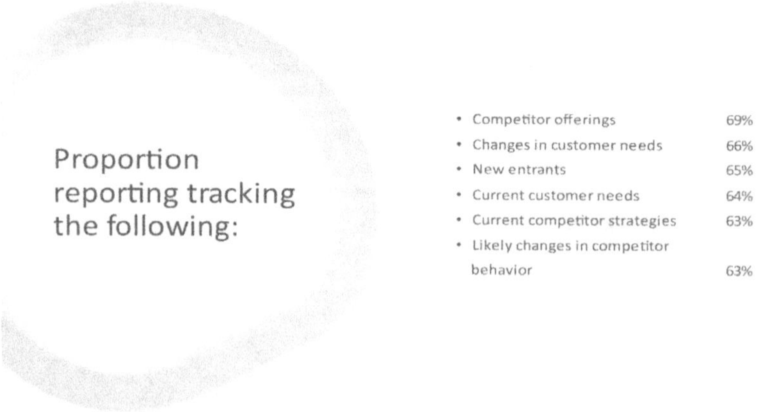

Figure 3: What companies call "competitive intelligence"

A simple comparison of Figures 2 and 3 should lead to a simple revelation: Closely tracking other players is insufficient to predict surprises and shifts in market dynamics caused by these players. Monitoring is not the same as market insights.

What's missing? What turns deliberate monitoring into market insights? The Big Picture is the most crucial framework to recognize and predict changing industry dynamics. But insight *doesn't show up on command.*

All opportunities (and risks) come from changing dynamics of power in an industry. Competitive intelligence, therefore, is based on learning to pick up early clues pointing to emerging changes in the Big Picture. If the clues are *obvious*, they are no longer viable as clues.

The Big Picture[7]

Michael Porter's depiction of the Big Picture came about when he looked at differential profitability across industries. Why is the software industry so much more profitable than hardware? Why are airlines' ROI so much lower than pharmaceutical companies? The best way to grasp the Big Picture and its importance in making companies find new growth opportunities is by visualizing it as a "tug of war" for the industry's "profit pool" among the various participants in the market.

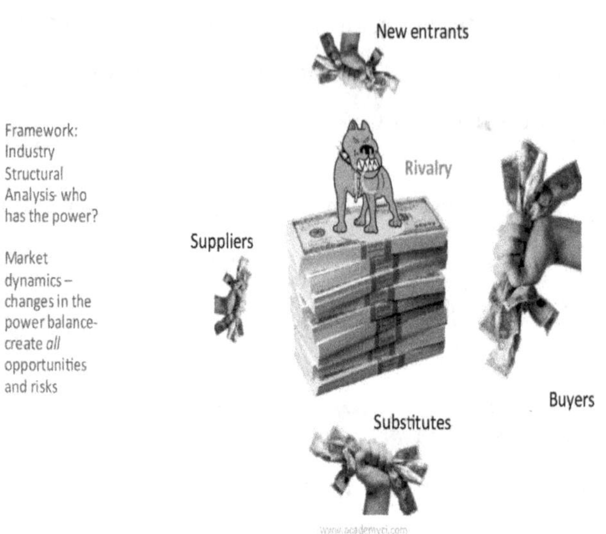

Figure 4: Industry structure as tag-of-war for a profit pool

Don't confuse tag-of-war imagery with actual war. Business is not war, though companies do "battle" each other in the market. They battle on price, features, location, etc. Tag-of-war is about relative power in grabbing a portion of the industry's profits. While bargaining with other market players such as buyers and distributors (the demand chain), regulators and suppliers (the supply chain), or substitutes (the disruption chain), competitors battle among themselves to gain a higher share of the profit. The ones with a competitive edge win a bigger share of the sector's profit (at least for a while.)

And then external developments called change drivers – technology, new regulations, social change, or new players - shift the balance of power. This balance is never constant. It always changes. Industries are not closed systems and are never in long-term equilibrium. That's why companies in their prospectus to investors state that past performance is *not* a guarantee of future performance.

If all market-facing personnel share a schema of the Big Picture and tune to signs the power is shifting due to a change driver, their collective wisdom can also shift top management perspective. A case in point below shows the power of changing paradigms.

<table>
<tr><td>

Case in point

In the 70s and into the 80s, pharmaceutical companies enjoyed very high returns based on the following industry dynamics:

- The enormous cost of developing a new drug (average of $900 million) deterred entry.

- The complicated demand chain - the users of drugs (patients) do not choose which medications to take, the prescribers of drugs (physicians) do not pay, the payer (insurance companies, the government) had limited bargaining power.

- Substitutions such as supplements, herbal remedies,or surgeries had limited effect on demand.

- Suppliers, except for research talent, sold mostly commodities (chemicals).

- Generics put a cramp in profit, but continuous innovation protected by patent laws and the endorsement of new rugs by leading physicians (Key Opinion Leaders) more than made up for it.

Then came biotech. Biotech research identified specific disease paths to target by complex molecules grown on living systems - organisms or plants, or cells. Before that, the discovery process was based on trial and error across millions of possible candidates - fully syntesized chemicals. While the production process for biologicals was way more expensive, there were no generic versions of biological

</td></tr>
</table>

drugs (complex molecules are hard to reproduce precisely). The discovery cost was as low as a few million in venture capital funding or JVs with university research labs.

Looking at Pharma's landscape and the major players - the Big Picture - back in the 80s, didn't reveal the enormous change that the substitution of synthesized chemicals with biotech molecules growing on living systems would bring. Traditional Pharma companies spent significant amounts on tracking industry developments from amazingly detailed prescription data (big and bigger) by such venerable vendors as IMS to a cocophony of consulting practices providing analysis and forecasts. Pharma being among the richest industries on earth, the consulting/market research/data space around it is filled to the brim with helpful data providers. Yet it was just one firm, Roche, which turned the noise into intelligence. The others just drowned in it.

Collaborating on research with the early pioneers in biotech, Genentech, during the 80s, Roche acquired 56% of the young company in 1990 for about $2 billion. At the time, analysts were shocked. Genentech had no revenues to speak of and no marketing or manufacturing capability. It mainly was "esoteric" R&D into recombinant DNA. So the move was considered a waste of resources[8]. Yet Roche's top executives' perspective was shaped by working with Genentech's founder's genius and seeing how it could change the industry. It took years to change perspective, and Roche didn't take immediate action except for the research collaboration. But when the perspective changed, Roche's top executives declared it to be *the future of Roche*, envisioning the industry's Big Picture changing dramatically over time. From a drying (traditional) pipeline to the rising cost of hospitalization (making even expensive biological drugs economical to payers), talent drain to small bio labs, and the promise of no generic competition to complex molecules, industry evolution was about to leap, and Roche was there *early*. In 2008, Roche paid $47 billion to complete its ownership of Genentech.

No degree of obsessively chasing prescription data would bring that $45 billion difference in valuation. Instead, it had to be a change in perspective brought about by competitive intelligence - a signal of things to come and options for a strategy that takes advantage of early opportunities.

Today most Pharma combine chemical and biotech divisions within their organization. For example, a former Genentech executive reporting directly to the CEO leads Roche's entire research.

Now that's using the Big Picture to turn noise into gold.

Quick takeaways for the road:

A shared platform for understanding the Big Picture helps companies harness the collective wisdom of managers' competitive intelligence.

Most important lesson for executives to learn from 25 years of spending millions on "monitoring the market", "tracking competitors", and so on?

Monitoring is not the same as competitive intelligence. Information is not insight.

PART I:
Transforming Data into Insight

Chapter 4:
Reading Other Players' Minds

Roche's success in reading the pharmaceutical industry's future started with a two-step process: Envisioning the evolution of the big picture *and* predicting other players' moves. In the above case, Roche realized the window of opportunity might close once other players started grabbing biotech companies. Thus, a first move advantage resulted in a low acquisition price (initially).

Predicting other players' moves and reactions comes at a price of a deliberate effort to understand third parties. To see the difference between sifting through the noise for signals of a power shift in the industry/segment - and *then* assessing other players' moves and reactions, we need to delve into how our brain uses attention to keep us alive.

Searching for opportunities requires an ability to sift through a lot of noise quickly and efficiently. Opportunities do not come with a label. The quest, therefore, cannot be systematic and labor-intensive. Discovering opportunities always involves an element of "serendipity." Such a quest seems to involve two distinct stages, described by Daniel Kahneman, Noble Prize winner in economics, as System 1 and System 2[9].

System 1 is an automatic scanning tool developed through evolutionary pressures to detect signs of change denoting possible risks or opportunities. The scanning is effortless and subconscious. We share this system with lots of other animals. System 2 is the analytical, deliberate attention to detail, the part of the brain that is energy consuming and requires effort. System 1 hands over a tidbit to System 2 *if it finds it needs further attention.*

***

Entrepreneurship, by definition, is based on the entrepreneur's belief that they discovered an opportunity (for profit). Entrepreneurship, therefore, *implies* the searcher's competitive intelligence quest. Every entrepreneurial venture starts with information deemed an opportunity for a business- be it a corner kiosk or Amazon. So how do entrepreneurs discover these opportunities?

In my doctoral research into entrepreneurship, I discovered only one "characteristic" that can explain such a search. Entrepreneurs exhibited *alertness* to opportunities[10]. Alertness means System 1 searching for them without conscious effort. Some people are searching for love; some are searching for meaning; activists are searching for power. Would-be entrepreneurs are searching for opportunities for an edge in the market.

What creates this specific alertness?

My research revealed that Locus of Control (LOC) had something to do with this alertness. Locus of Control is an old concept in psychology (originating in 1954's work by Julian Rotter). It is the belief in your ability to control outcomes. Internal LOC means you believe you can shape reality to some extent. External LOC is a belief that what happens is totally outside your control. There is empirical evidence that internal LOC in entrepreneurs is higher than the general population – as expected- but I also found evidence for internal LOC relations with perceptual alertness, a concept in neuroscience.

Since competing implies using specific information to gain an edge, some internal LOC is a prerequisite by default. The opposite, external LOC means a belief in luck or divine intervention or other people's control of outcomes. One hypothesis is that internal LOC motivates System 1 to search for opportunities in the noise since pursuing an opportunity requires *some* sense of control over results.

But that's about it. Internal LOC doesn't guarantee that your search yields meaningful results. Paradoxically, believing in your ability to achieve your goals, shape the outcome, and take advantage of an opportunity, also entails reckoning with the fact that achieving that outcome depends on predicting other parties' reactions.

For people who believe in luck, there is no need to understand third parties. Everything is outside their control. Some luck is inevitable even for people with internal LOC, but it is possible to reduce the reliance on luck with some planning. Part of this planning is envisioning the moves and countermoves of parties that can influence the outcome. While competitive intelligence is information used to gain a competitive edge, the notion of "other players" is embedded in the term, *competitive.*

The fundamental principle of this book is that when we compete, those who understand the value of market insight fare better. Thus, assuming you are only interested in ethical competition (not using deceit or coercion), considering other players' perspectives, predicting their moves and reactions, and asking, "how can I take advantage of it?" should be part of conceiving an edge.

If you understand that finding the gold nugget in the massive noise around you is aided by deliberate effort to predict third parties' moves and reactions, you may ask yourself: Am I up to this task? Doesn't it require deep business knowledge, financial expertise, and a seasoned record in an industry?

The answer is not a simple yes or no.

Market-facing managers come from numerous business areas: marketing, strategy, business development, tech, sales, and research functions are some examples. Thus, the specific functional background is immaterial to joining the competitive intelligence quest.

The skills of "reading" shifts in markets, outlined in Chapter 3, don't require a Ph.D. in quantum mechanics to grasp. Educational background is immaterial. We've trained brilliant librarians who wanted to transition from archiving to an active quest for intelligence, as well as PhDs in life sciences and geniuses in software development and graduates of liberal arts in college. We've trained MBAs from top schools and BAs from state colleges. They shared an interest in developing market insights, not just shuffling around data and information.

Assessing and predicting other players' moves and reactions requires one predilection: The desire to dig beneath the surface. At times, experience in the industry helps. At times, it hampers. Curiosity, the hallmark of "digging beneath the surface," is fickle.

Since System 2 is conscious and deliberate, it is also trainable. One must keep in mind just two principles when assessing and predicting third parties' moves and reactions.

First principle: *Basic* economics

All industries run on economics. The economics of an industry determines who survives and who fails. It is inescapable, just like deficits and printing money don't create real growth, and curtailing oil drilling raises the price of fuel. Economics 101 *always* wins.

Many managers who are not well-versed in economics believe it is a series of math equations and statistical models based on unrealistic assumptions beyond their grasp. How much economics did you study in college if you have a liberal art degree or even a marketing degree? And if you studied economics, how much of it was relevant to your job?

The reality is very different. Economics has many versions, and the dominant one, known as Neoclassical, is by no means the best one for you to understand. The intrusion of math into economics in the 60s replaced basic economic thinking, known as classical economics, with jargon and ever more sophisticated statistical models. Classical economics, on the other hand, has superior value for a manager in a business.

Fundamental (classical) economic thinking works through a theory- a logical construct based on everyday observations- not statistical ad hoc models. The latter often prove far less reliable than other similar models in physical science.

There are naturally many sources for anyone interested in economics, but the knowledge that one needs is of two kinds:

1. General (classical) economic principles- universal and self-explanatory
2. Specific economics of your industry/segment.

On the first kind, my recommendation is to read a short, eye-opening, down-to-earth paper titled: How I became a Libertarian[11]. The author, Prof. Meir Kohn is s mathematician at the business school at Dartmouth University, so his credentials are impeccable. His theory belongs to a body of work called "Austrian economics" based on its origin with classical economists in Austria back in the early 20th century. This school of thought has proved better at predicting economic outcomes than sophisticated neoclassical models.

In Kohn's theory, three forces shape our economic reality: production, commerce, and government. It is the interaction between these forces that determine how markets evolve. Thus, assessing how these three factors are trending facilitates predicting the likely change drivers in any given industry's evolution. The three forces, production, commerce, and government, encapsulate technology, regulation, social and new competitors identified in Chapter 3 as directly impacting an industry's power balance.

The specific economic forces working in one's segment/industry do require managers to understand the "success factors" in their industry. Still, most managers with a few years of working in an industry are intuitively aware of these factors. A few fundamental factors such as economies of scale (the reduction in your cost when the volume of an activity such as production increases), network externalities (the change in the value of service or product when the number of users increases), first-mover advantage, and similar simple concepts are applicable in all industries at different stages of their evolution.

These "success factors" are driven by the basic economics of capacity utilization, fixed vs. variable costs, price elasticity, buyers' switching cost, and so on. In the long run, they will always- always- make or break a company. But in the short run, economic considerations often give way to more nuanced behavioral-economic principles: the intersection of psychology, politics, history, culture, etc., with the economic reality. I cover behavioral economics in the next section.

While classic economic principles will help a manager grasp the Big Picture, two other principles of classical economics help predict individual companies' behaviors.

Economics 101: The two most important principles for assessing and predicting other players' moves and reactions are as follows:
1. There is no free lunch
2. Incentives do work! (a.k.a follow the money)

There is no free lunch

Is a simple principle warns that what looks too good to be true is indeed just that. It also warns to always look for the unintended consequence of government intervention in the market, either through regulations, taxation, or directed investment (e.g., subsidies). The idea that quantitative easing (printing money) by Trump and Biden will not result in inflation is the idea that there is a free lunch.

"Incentives do work" is a popular (and very valid) approach in both criminal investigations and assessing and predicting other players' moves and reactions. For example, companies' market behavior can be traced to how their executives are incentivized, how their sales force is paid, or how divisions compete or cooperate for resources inside the parent company.

Case in Point
A little known anecdote from Steve Jobs' history at Apple is that he refused to organize Apple by business units' P&L when he returned to save the company. Instead, he put the company on one P&L, a strategy followed by his successor, Tim Cook, to this day.   This unique financial system came to forte when Epic - a game developer - sued Apple in court for refusing to include its App in Apple's store. Asking to see the store's profitability, Tim Cook had an easy reply: we are not organized that way; we don't track expenses back to the store[12]. Instead, the various functions (Apple no longer has business units) are incentivized based on the company's overall health, and there is no separate allocation of cost to each product.

> The rationale, which worked well for Apple (but may *not* work for others), was to prevent functions from fighting over cost allocation. Instead, the objective was to incentivize them to focus on the customer.

Second principle: Companies have character

Understanding other players' strategy, however, has little to do with a straightforward understanding of economics. Companies' behavior is a strange mixture of history, personalities, drivers, and assumptions. Some see reality; some see virtual reality. Some have visions of a future that come true, and some have double visions. Thus, delving into the mindsets of third parties (competitors, large customers, partners, or other influential players) is not a straightforward analysis like a basic understanding of the economics of industries.

The issue of training your System 2 in the second stage of the competitive intelligence quest is therefore not a matter of high IQ or an MBA. Instead, it's a matter of how comfortable a person is with nonlinear thinking. Nonlinear thinking expands the horizon of your alertness from "what is happening" (System 1) to "where is the opportunity" (System 2).

Getting into other players' minds

As a manager automatically scans the landscape for clues about opportunities, they might come across a bit that they think will give their company an advantage. Whatever it is, their System 2 kicks in and reckons with the fact that success is never entirely up to the company and that without understanding other players' perspectives on this "opportunity" and their potential moves, the executives might be just creating a wishful world.

The competitive intelligence quest requires a "walk" in someone else's brains. Not shoes- these can be replaced in a heartbeat. Brains can't.

From the industry structure (Figure 4), you already know there are at least five categories of high-impact players affecting your company's fortunes. Each of them brings its perspective about the evolution of the segment/industry/market. The more you understand others' perspectives, the higher the probability an opportunity is real.

There are many models for analyzing a company. I am biased towards Michael Porter's four-corner model, adapted for my training as follows.

The behavioral-economic framework for stepping into someone else's shoes: Don't confuse cause and effect

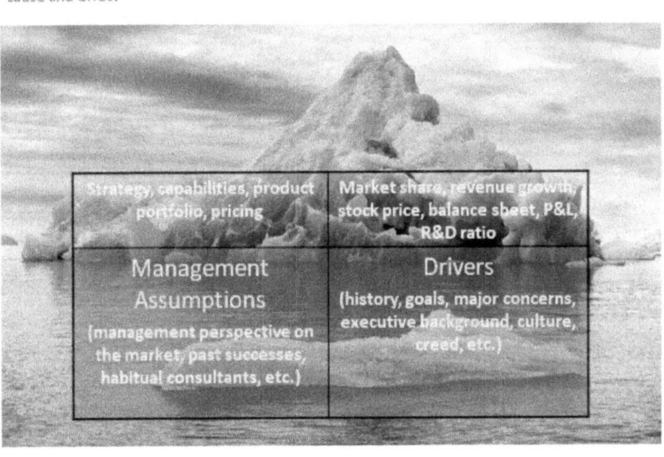

Figure 5: Understanding High Impact Players

Understanding the perspective of other players – whether competitors, large customers, regulatory agencies, politicians, or "disruptors" can sometimes be challenging (if the party is foreign), or it can turn out relatively easy. In either case, what's hidden "under the surface" is way more significant than what marketing communications or CEOs' press conferences state.

Case in Point

Let's role-play a large forestry company like Weyerhaeuser. You own 11 million acres of forests in the US and lease 14 million more in Canada. You sell a lot of wood to the construction industry since the favorite house frame in the US is a wood frame. Why? History, cost, tradition.

Then lumber prices start rising. As lumber prices soar in one year alone (300-400% in 2021) and despite some economists (e.g., Paul Kruger) claiming this is temporary, you know the truth: A run-up in lumber prices has been in the making for years. Are you happy? Any time demand rises sharply, and you can charge more, while your cost doesn't rise as much, your earnings are going to be a delight.

Too steep a rise, however, is never a good thing. That's because people are going to start looking for alternatives (substitutes in Figure 4).

A reputable source (Time) publishes an article calling for people to increase the use of steel and concrete in building houses. You firmly believe wood is a better product for building houses, and the market proves it by making wood frame houses the dominant choice. In 2019, 90% of all houses were wood-frame houses. BUT---steel and especially concrete houses are a worthy substitute. They are sturdier, more energy-efficient, have lower maintenance, etc. The number of concrete frame houses has increased by 46% from 2018 to 2019, while wood-frame increased by 8% only.[13]

So what do you do? First, you, of course, deny that concrete is better than wood. But behind closed doors, I expect you make different speeches. Most likely, you start to look for an alternative use for your forests.

A story out of California suggests that forests are becoming an essential element in the state's climate change policies. This is because forests absorb more CO_2 than they release. Therefore, if you are an environmental zealot (CA is), they can come into play nicely in earning carbon credits which you can then turn around and sell to polluting industries. According to an article in MIT Technology Review, Indian tribes, in particular, found a nice niche like that. Using statistical averaging of various types of trees (not all trees absorb the same level of carbon) to game the system, they have earned underserving credits and made millions selling them. Entrepreneurship knows no bounds. Kudos.

If you are a large forestry company, like Weyerhaeuser, you are quick to note this little scheme. Forests are becoming a gold mine not just for harvesting them but for not harvesting them and looking to gain carbon credits. Imagine this wonderful government-incentivized world were not doing something makes you more money than doing it. This is Alice in Wonderland or, more accurately, Alice in California. The only issue is when and where you don't harvest since the opportunity cost of not harvesting (i.e., the revenue from an alternative action) must be lower. So, you keep an eye out for government policies that will change the equation.

In a year or two, I won't be surprised to read that Weyerhaeuser is now the biggest seller of carbon credits, and it hasn't cut one tree anywhere in California.

Looking at the world from someone's else perspective is not rocket science. It's behavioral economic science[14]. You don't have to be right all the time, just enough times to see an opportunity.

It's impossible not to be utterly impressed with the unequivocal victory of Netflix over its main competitors in a crowded field of entertainment streaming, especially Amazon. Netflix doesn't only teach us about algorithm limitations (see Chapter 9). It teaches us a lesson in gaining an edge with just a tiny bit of data but a consistent and determined strategy.

Amazon's Prime Video streaming has lost the war with Netflix. From a formidable "existential threat" to Netflix back in 2007, Amazon Prime has dropped below HBO Max, Hulu, and so far behind Netflix, it is just "one more" competitor.

Netflix's attained total victory with a deliberate decision to gain an edge in original content. While Amazon has as many titles and earlier had many more titles than Netflix, Netflix correctly predicted that amazon's focus would not be on original productions but on acquiring and leveraging its extensive library. The reason is Netflix's vision of content creation contrasts with Amazon's roots in a long tail of thinking from the retail side as Prime is just another service to subscribers. Moreover, Amazon Video's parent company focuses on AWS, the cloud platform, where Amazon's profitability resides and where it fights with much larger competitors (Microsoft, Google, Oracle).

Anticipating Amazon's focus being elsewhere and predicting it will be reluctant to get into a protracted and expensive battle for original content, Netflix massively outproduced Amazon in what in the industry is called "certified fresh content." As a result, Amazon Prime Video just basically died.

There is a lesson in this example to strategists: You don't have to be genuinely innovative- opportunities do not spell breakthrough science, shocking discoveries, or whole new strategy. Netflix's original films are bad. Really bad. Not an original thought in sight except producing in "exotic" locations/languages like Polish, Russian, Portuguese, Korean, and Hebrew. Maybe it's cheaper. Perhaps it expands viewership (though most Americans hate reading subtitles). The point is an opportunity for an edge might be present in simply overwhelming the competition. It's a legitimate winning proposition under certain circumstances (of course, you need to understand the role of circumstances, and that's why spotting opportunities is so much more complex than mere data dumps.)

Let me sum up what a manager needs for a competitive intelligence quest or market insight about an opportunity (applies equally well to risks):

1. Be alert to signals of change in the Big Picture.

   If you keep in mind that all opportunities (and risks) emerge from changing power balance in your market/ segment/industry, your brain will do the rest automatically. Once you are good at the construction of the Big Picture, your brain will know what to look for: any nugget that signals a possible change from the status quo.

2. When your System 1 is intrigued by a contradiction between what you expected to see/hear/read, it will alert System 2. You may want to deliberately search for more data on the incongruity.

3. System 2 then assesses and predicts other players' moves and reactions, setting "boundaries" on the potential opportunity.

Do not look for accuracy or tactical details this early in the intelligence quest. Instead, just sketch out the opportunity the way you perceive it. On what does it depend? Which other players are significant for it to materialize?

4. Once you have some context to what System 1 noticed, communicate with others who might be able to add to your understanding.
5. Translate the perceived opportunity into strategy options for the company.
6. Communicate to management (more of that in part III).

Quick takeaways for the road:

> *Competing requires training your mind, not changing your personality!*

> *Economics 101: The two most important principles for assessing and predicting other players' moves and reactions:*
>
> 1. *There is no free lunch*
> 2. *Incentives do work! (a.k.a follow the money)*

> *The more you understand others' perspectives, the higher the probability and opportunity is real.*

Chapter 5: Demonstrating the Power

Most decision makers couldn't care less about the difference between data, information, and intelligence because they believe such distinctions have minor practical implications for them.

They should care.

Information is a commodity. Everyone has it; competitors share the same information by using the same sources- industry reports, consultants' white papers, databases, and news aggregators (so-called "platforms").

Intelligence is what gives a company the edge over other players.

Managers may read the same piece of information but come to very different conclusions. For example, while ninety-nine out of a hundred managers reading a market study just put it down to "good to know," one manager picks up an intriguing tidbit. It's in that manager's interpretation of this tidbit that all opportunities lie.

To demonstrate the difference beyond an abstract definition and a practical use, let me take you through the journey from a tidbit or datum to full competitive intelligence (market insight). I've chosen items I picked when I opened my Edge browser (a very appropriate name for my purposes) during one week in late April 2021. These examples reflect my personal interests. This is precisely the point: A tiny bit of information pops into our field of vision when we find it intriguing, and we find it intriguing if it is incongruent with expectations, and that incongruity may have some value for us. Otherwise, we just skim over it, ignore it, or maybe catalog it for routine use and move on.

Corollary 4: Intelligence is not "objective" since opportunities are not objective. They always serve the agenda of the user.

Figures 6 and 7 below visualize the cognitive *journey* of a piece of datum all the way to becoming market insight signaling a potential opportunity.

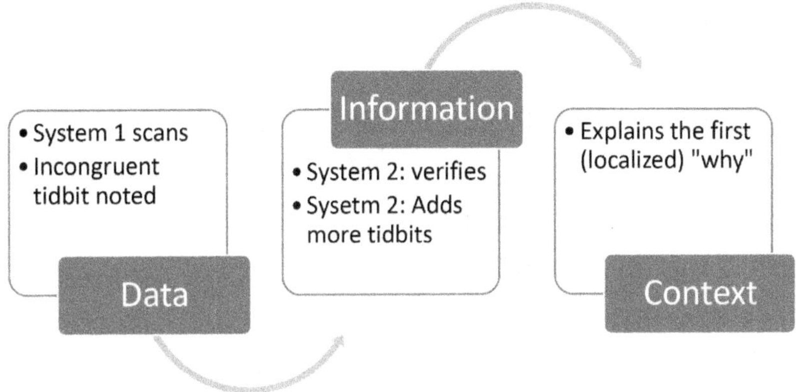

Figure 6: The journey of tidbit to context

Figure 7: Context turns into an opportunity (can you spot it?)

The journey

The beginning of the journey is a datum "tidbit."

On April 28, 2021, reports emerged that Project Veritas sued CNN for defaming it on air. Project Veritas is an anti-corruption organization that uses a hidden camera to document unethical behavior and organizations. In 2021, Twitter banned Project Veritas from its platform.

According to court documentation, CNN claimed *on-air* that Twitter banned Veritas because "like many right-wing sources, it provided misinformation." It turns out Twitter banned Project Veritas for violating privacy rules by recording CNN's senior staffer's admission regarding CNN's biased reporting. Tomayto-tomhato? Maybe. But it may result in CNN paying a lot of tomatoes.

Let's role play. Say you are an editor or a marketing manager at Fox News, competing with CNN for viewership. The first step in the journey of the tidbit is you *notice this lawsuit.*

Many people will read this tidbit and pay no attention, moving on to more exciting tidbits (to them).

From datum to information

The first step in noticing a tidbit starts by *being intrigued.*

What is the basis for all attention to opportunities? Incongruity with the current perspective of how things work and why. If what you observe (read, hear, or see) is congruent with what you expect, you move on. System 1 – the automatic scanning tool developed through evolution to detect signs of change denoting possible risks or opportunities doesn't refer anything to System 2 – the deliberate and "costly" effort of analysis- unless it is of interest, and incongruency always is. If the world is as you expect, the tidbit is just part of the background hum.

However, an intelligent manager at Fox News should be intrigued by CNN's careless behavior on the air. It is not typical. CNN prides itself on being professional. CNN has many good journalists. System 1 then hands over this tidbit to System 2. The Fox news marketer's System 2, the analytical attention to detail energy-consuming cognitive process first checks to see if the report is accurate. Maybe it's the infamous "fake news"? Verifying reliability by looking for other sources and cross-referencing, she finds out indeed, CNN's on-air claim was false. The datum becomes information (verified data).

The Fox manager's journey to competitive insight starts by asking herself: Why was CNN so careless? What she came across did not explain that. To understand a specific event at a particular point in time (i.e., put it in *context*), she may need to gather more data.

System 2's journey from information to intelligence proceeds with a simple question: *Why?*

In this case: Why has CNN lost its professional reporting standards?

This first WHY is the moment information is no longer sufficient. Competitive intelligence quest uses lots of "why."

In reaction to the "why," our Fox marketer searches for more data to put the event *in context*. Data without context is lonely data. Since this is a search to explain a particular event, the search is "localized." What was it that made CNN so touchy?

Added bits: CNN has been bleeding viewers in the charged partisan environment of "news" post the 2020 elections. With President Trump out of office, non-partisan viewers no longer valued CNN's trump card (pun intended).

Added bits: Project Veritas recorded a CNN staffer admitting the network was deliberately promoting propaganda. That was a breakthrough for the Project Veritas organization.

Context: The video recorded by Project Veritas will exacerbate CNN's biased reporting image, a notion popularized by President Trump and supported by media watch companies. Such revelations may cost it dearly with middle-of-the-road independent viewers. That makes Project Veritas' latest success a "hot button" for CNN. Hot buttons push companies to react strongly, often out of reasonable proportion. So, while CNN was able to laugh off Project Veritas' sneaky sensational videos in the past, this one struck a nerve. CNN stumbled.

We use aggregating data with other data to *explain* what's happening in a specific situation (localized context). This explanation requires an *"interpreter"* moving away from data and into context.

Turning context into insight

Recall that we are role-playing a marketer at Fox News, CNN's bitter rival. Looking at the Big Picture using the framework presented in Chapter 3 and searching for an opportunity for Fox News as CNN is stumbling will turn the tidbit into competitive intelligence (market insight).

What is the Big Picture? First, let's look at the whole news segment of the media industry. There is a significant rise in the power of social networks, as more and more viewers get their news exclusively off them (55% as of 2019). As a result, rivalry in the diminished pie of TV News segment of the media industry is turning fierce.

How do the various news outlets compete? The strategy of partisan networks such as MSNBC and Fox News is to gravitate towards selective reporting (*not* fake news but careful selection of what to feature) to serve their base. Both have been growing fast. CNN has been caught in the middle, attempting to play the "center" game, in a vanishing center that depends on an impeccable image of balanced reporting. With several scandals (such as not covering Governor Cuomo's COVID coverup as his brother is a powerful CNN star, and conservative documented claims of Trump Derangement Syndrome at the network), CNN's image has been destroyed. Even sympathetic partisan outlets like The Washington Post declared CNN to turn more emotional than professional.

With Trump gone, CNN lost a lot of its emotional appeal. Though CNN delivers revenue (profit data aren't made public by its parent company), it lags badly behind Fox News. Warner Media, its corporate owner, is a division within AT&T that includes many other media assets (such as HBO Max). This division is diverting cash from AT&T's focus on 5G. If I am AT&T, a business company, not overly partisan, CNN's growing stumbles might be the last straw that pushes me to look for ways out.

Strengthening substitutes (social media), intensifying rivalry (NSNBC and Fox News), declining viewership, and the rising power of buyers as they switch easily to other news sources are shifting the balance of power in this industry's segment of News away from venerable legacy networks like CNN. This shift offers the opportunity for Fox News to hammer as much as possible precisely on this point of *credibility*. The two networks have condemned each other as biased or fake news for years now, but Project Veritas' recording is the first time CNN was caught publicly editorializing content to manipulate perceptions. Thus, project Veritas' trial- if it goes to trial, which is rather unlikely - is an excellent opportunity for Fox to hit CNN where it hurts. If I were Fox's people, I'd contribute privately to Project Veritas' legal fund and push for a public trial.

Quite often, "hot buttons" serve to direct tactical moves to achieve an edge by finding chink in the competitor's armor. The loss of cool at CNN offers ample tactical options to push its hot buttons further, given the rising pressures in the News segment of the media industry.

Update: In May 2021, AT&T announced the jettisoning of Warner Media to Discovery, a programing company owner of Animal Planets, Oprah Show, and HGTV, among other non-scripted programs. In this sale, AT&T will lose a huge chunk of money.

With the new owner, CNN may see an expansion of *non*-news programs as the News segment is seen more a burden than an asset. For one, CNN's Parts Unknown with Antony Bourdain was a successful move away from the declining reputation of the News division. Project Veritas' trial may be the nail in the coffin, and Fox News may widen its lead beyond repair as viewers split between Fox and MSNBC, the two unabashedly partisan networks.

If you like CNN, this is not good news. If you don't like CNN, this is excellent news. Either way, a tiny bit of information about a lawsuit transformed into a prediction of a high-impact player's (AT&T) move before it happened and led to a market insight opening an opportunity for cementing the consolidation of the news media behind only two networks.

Befitting the toxic culture war in the US, CNN may become a sideshow on Animal Planet.

Quick takeaways for the road:

> *Users don't care about the distinction between information and intelligence. They should. Treating every bit of information as important is as bad as treating all information as useless.*

> *All real intelligence quests start with the first WHY.*

> *Context: Putting bits of information together to explain an event that is incongruent with what one expects.*

> *Data alone is GIGO. More data, big data can be more and bigger GIGO (Garbage-In, Garbage-Out). Only context gives relevance to data.*

PART II:

Obstacles in the Competitive Intelligence Hunt

Chapter 6:
From Data-driven to
Data-drivel?

Some readers may confuse the competitive intelligence quest with data-driven decisions.

It is nothing like that.

For many untrained eyes, data and intelligence are the same. According to IDC, a research company, data traffic on the internet will reach 175 zettabytes in 2025. Just for comparison's sake, since most of us know a few gigabytes as our dream storage in the cloud or on our memory card, a zettabyte is one *trillion* gigabytes.

Impressive, isn't it?

Competitive intelligence, however, is the *tiniest tiny* portion of these zettabytes that will have any meaningful effect on a company's future. That tiny portion has no positive linear relationship to the *amount* of data a company collects, stores, and disseminates internally. In fact, it may have a negative relationship as noise masks insights.

Data-driven decisions are in vogue, but they are limited to an attempt to better execute existing strategy (think better-targeted ads on Facebook). Opportunities, by default, are based on signals that precede lots of data. By the time Big Data is available, a company may lose an opportunity for a first-mover advantage that shapes its future. What will be left is better execution as companies converge on the same growth patterns discovered by data analytics.

With a lack of substantial data behind them, opportunities are based on intuition, a sense of where things are going, and an imagination of future industry structures where the power balance has shifted. Current research suggests that intuition is based on learning from experience, but the experience can be idiosyncratic (unique to the individual), at times random (serendipitous), and therefore experience is not synonymous with lots of data. The *amount* of *available* data is unrelated to the success of the competitive intelligence quest.

Unlike data-based (reactive) decisions, the sphere of proactive decisions supposes using a few early signals of change to come- not the whole picture. When the picture is clear, one is merely *reacting*.

Naturally, when asked, CEOs claim they intend to push for more data-driven culture in their organization. This is understandable. If data-driven decisions improve the execution of existing strategies, they are beneficial. They allow companies to "stay in the game."

However, when Blockbuster realized Netflix was not just a curiosity and tried to "stay in the DVD by mail" game, it was too late. Staying in the game might be necessary, but it is not sufficient to create an edge. It may buy a company time, but it may find itself behind if it uses that time to collect more data.

The culture of "worshipping" data would be of minimal significance if not for the detrimental effect on a company's cadre of market-facing managers. As top management insists on "more data," it misses out on early signs, first moves, and a longer-lasting advantage.

Opportunities come from competitive intelligence quest- signals of things to come, not evidence things have already passed one over.

Back in the 20th century, Peter Drucker said companies' main asset was their knowledge. He didn't mean data. Unfortunately, the transition from data to knowledge is far from simple, and most companies fail to do it well.

Another pitfall to focusing on data is that some consultants attempt to rid companies of real strategies altogether and instead point to data-driven decisions as the way to reach their goals. This is a risky move. Data-directed strategies, according to this bad advice, should change when data change. Unfortunately, this confuses refinements to an existing strategy with getting ahead of other players by pursuing new strategic opportunities.

Competing requires thinking ahead, speculating, imagining, listening to the "voice of the market." Alertness to signals of possible changes in the Big Picture doesn't require attention to details or accuracy.

While data-driven decisions have a vital role in fine-tuning activities, creating a fetish about data is dangerous. The insecurity of managers drives out intuition as it calls out for more data.

The Muppets have a new puppet. It eats cookie monster for lunch. It then burps more data.

The "data revolution"

To fully grasp the difference between data-driven decisions and the competitive intelligence quest, one needs to look no further than... decisions of how to digitalize. Today's urgent strategic decision is about the *route* to the digitalization of operations by which Big Data delivers better service in many industries. Yet, ironically, data themselves have little relevance to the *strategy* of digitalization.

Companies jumping on the wagon of digitalization need to decide how to approach this big project. What is the best route to digitalization? A company can follow other players in its market. It can choose to leapfrog and lead other players. Once a company makes that decision, it needs to follow it with a further decision (sometimes simultaneous with the first) regarding developing in-house or buying the technology. If it embarks on buying it, the consideration shifts to best of breed or eco-system strategy. There are pros and cons to each approach and in the end, what companies decide depends on what they believe will best give them an edge in the future. This decision, in turn, requires some speculation as to what competitors will choose, and customers prefer, and so on. There are no data about that yet. If there were an optimal route, it wouldn't be a strategic decision, would it? Companies will simply make a tactical choice of "buy vs. grow" based on straightforward financial consideration.

When there aren't enough data, one leaps. Companies leap.

Competing requires a leap as the future is never certain, enough data are never available, and if they are, it's often too late for a real opportunity. For creating an edge, only a tiny portion of the available data is relevant as early signals. Since predictive analytics requires thousands if not millions of observations, it can never be an *early* signal.

This simple logic sometimes escapes companies who insist on "we need more data" while simultaneously pushing for more agility. However, the logic doesn't escape the entrepreneurs.

Case in Point: Zoom vs. Webex

Zoom was created by Eric Yuan, a Chinese immigrant to the US who joined Webex in 1997. Webex was a small company working on software for real-time collaboration. Cisco bought Webex in 2007, and Yuan became Corporate Vice President for Engineering in charge of collaboration software. In his job, he met with customers. Not millions, not even thousands- probably several dozens. They didn't like their collaboration solutions, including Cisco's Webex solution.

Cisco is a great company. It has been a true engine of innovation and the backbone of the internet revolution. But Cisco is not one company- it's an amalgamation of dozens of business units, hundreds of product lines, all competing for corporate resources. Cisco didn't pay much attention to the real-time collaboration business. It wasn't a priority for the company. There wasn't a great demand for video conferencing calls, and big data didn't exist yet to support a notion that customers were placing priorities on real-time teamwork. Unified communication that combines communication of real-time (phone calls) and not real-time (emails, messages, etc.) and stores it for later retrieval was a bigger business. Market research reports and Gartner didn't point out that the real-time, cloud-based video/audio collaboration is where the opportunities lie.

So, in 2011, Yuan left Cisco to start Zoom. The rest is history.

Today, Cisco's Webex, the pioneer in collaboration software, is in an urgent dash to try and catch up to Zoom, Microsoft Teams, Google Meet, and other platforms. Sure, COVID and remote working made real-time collaboration platforms a priority for many companies, but the early signals missed by Cisco and noted by Yuan didn't need COVID or data to see the future.

Large companies wait for and spend millions on expensive rearview-mirror research reports; Entrepreneurs and agile competitors just leap, envisioning a changing Big Picture.

The unspoken *ceteris paribus* trap most people are unaware of

You can teach a machine to produce more efficiently with digital controls; you can even eliminate labor altogether; you can create APIs that follow people to their grave and beyond (talk about digital hell), but you can't automate executives' strategic decisions, which invariably imply unknown probabilities or payoffs. These require foresight, and foresight implies bolder imagination and courage, not more data. Data are invariably, inevitably, about what happened yesterday, extrapolated to tomorrow, ceteris paribus, economists' fancy term for All Else Being Equal when the reality is never actually All Else Being Equal.

Driving with a rear-view mirror is no way to avoid collision with the reality of being late.

Tapping into a network of market-facing employees with perspectives on a changing Big Picture requires management that realizes discontinuities prevent better predictions from analytics. In laymen's terms, it means models can't see surprises coming; only managers can.

Big picture vs. more data

In "war games" or strategy-pressure workshops, predicting other players' moves and reactions is paramount to developing realistic and robust strategic options. A product can be superior, and a company loses—for example, IBM's operating stem against DOS. A product can be lousy, and a company wins. Example: Microsoft's Internet Explorer. Service offering can be terrible, and a company still wins. Example: Facebook/Twitter/Bumble/ all other algorithmic-reliant companies. Service can be first-rate, and a company loses—for example, your small local pharmacy. The assumptions competitors and customers make about what's important in the Big Picture raise or lower their bargaining power, and that affects a company defining and pursuing an opportunity.

<table>
<tr><td>

Case in Point

Take, for example, Netflix. Everyone is familiar with the narrative of Reed Hastings beating Blockbuster, first on customer experience and then in using available technology. However, it is less apparent how Netflix keeps its edge in an age where there are more streaming services than good content. Have you ever heard of Tubi? Fubo? Crackle? Philo?!?

If you are a product manager at Netflix, competing with Amazon Prime, what should you do? You can run for the hills (Amazon devours everything around), or you can think- how will rivalry change? Which Big Picture's element will become different as competition intensifies that much? *Where is the opportunity?*

Full disclosure: I never worked with Netflix. This is just my thinking. Role-playing a marketing manager at Netflix back in 2011 when Amazon added 5,000 titles to its Prime Video service, I am thinking: This is just the beginning. First, we have more titles, then they have more titles, then... etc. Let's look at the Big Picture: Amazon Prime

</td></tr>
</table>

will not be the last streaming service. What will change in the Big Picture? Naturally, competition. But that's trivial. What is going to happen next? The enormous quantity of content is going to desensitize customers. While our (Netflix) vast library of content was an advantage initially, this edge is being eliminated. Too much noise.

Then sometimes passes, more noise, more competition, and somewhere out there you come across a bit suggesting that people *don't like too many choices.* It might have been reported in Psychology Today or an anti-capitalism opinion column by a regressive activist or academic research that had nothing to do with you, your company, or your industry.

You can spend millions on sophisticated market research to report back to management the breakthrough perspective that consumers are getting confused by too many titles. Unfortunately, that's the rearview mirror. Or you can intuitively recognize that and ask: How can I take advantage of *my perspective* on things to come? And what will my competitors do?

Prediction: Amazon most likely will use viewers' star-rating system. That is a classic Amazon's creed carried over from the retail operation.

So, Netflix doesn't use it. Instead, Netflix uses a popularity ranking: Number 1-10 "choice of viewers" at any moment in time. Why? Because people will be curious to see what others find so appealing. Network externality.

If you wait for data to determine strategy, you don't have a strategy to begin with.

The intelligence angle in compete

Are you familiar with the acronym VUCA? It stands for volatility, uncertainty, complexity, and ambiguity. It is supposed to describe our current world. Yet if you work for a living, you should know the real meaning: Virtually Useless Catchy Acronym. It is used by those selling you more noise to prey on your natural tendency to feel more in control of the environment by accumulating more noise. It's your amygdala speaking- the instinctive fear of the unknown bred for evolutionary purposes.

Do we truly think the Phoenician trader 3,000 years ago lived in a world of certainty? How about the caveman venturing out to hunt a mammoth?

If you are on a competitive intelligence quest, ignore data. Yes, you heard right: *Ignore data.* You need to know the difference between the operational use of more data to improve efficiency and the inherent, unremovable uncertainty of strategic decisions that no amount of data will ever alleviate because you have been left behind by the time enough data exist.

Instead of looking for more and bigger data, more certainty, and easy solutions, managers must shift their focus to a different mindset. They should automatically match every byte crossing their desk, every zettabyte processed by their tired brains against the following question: Can we use it to gain an edge as a company?

The answer depends on the following comparison, which managers should make with little conscious effort as a company deploys a shared platform of the Big Picture thinking: Compared with the current state of power balance in our market, how will this move the needle? The next step is a more conscious analysis (so-called System 2): Does it give rise to a new opportunity? What are the options? Which one is best for the company?

Imagine the value in hundreds of market-facing managers of a typical large company sharing a mindset of competitive intelligence quest, nurtured, and encouraged by their company.

If only top management recognized that value.

<table><tr><td>

Case in Point: Fighting COVID 19

There is little doubt *data* served to inform or misinform many of the strategies used to contain the COVID epidemic. The scientific reliance on data-driven decisions meant decisions used more and more data. The problem started when decisions were made under that disguise but for which the data *had no relevance.*

The spectacular failure of some epidemiological COVID models (the infamous Ferguson model in the UK) should have given big data/predictive analytics advocates a pause in their step. But, instead, they doubled down.

The COVID epidemic of 2020 provided us with an unfortunate lens through which we can view the difference between data-driven and data-drivel. Even the most hyped-up "data-driven strategies" of fighting COVID in 2020-2021 were more panic-driven than data-driven. Masks or no masks; social distance or exceptions for protests; shutdowns or Sweden; open schools or kill the economy. None of these decisions could have been based on the available data alone. The reason is not that we didn't have enough data- the standard excuse of subject experts' narrow perspective. Instead, the decisions required grasping the Big Picture, reckoning with "we'll never have enough data," weighing on various alternatives, considering economic, psychological, sociological, and medical issues, which was impossible for self-preserving politicians.

I don't blame the politicians. I blame the consensus that more data lead to better decisions. If companies carry this mindset to competition in a (relatively) free market, people who advocate for more data risk missing the train.

</td></tr></table>

Most executives are experienced enough and busy enough to know what indeed is helpful for their strategic decisions. In politics, politicians knew what was beneficial to keep their fearful base happy. That had nothing to do with data-driven decisions. It had to do with ideology, instincts, populist assumptions, and looking to keep the edge in the next election cycle. And we don't have data yet (as of 2021) if their premises were correct. Did the lockdown work for them politically? Yes, no, we'll know in 2022. Was shutting down millions of businesses and killing the livelihood of millions of workers necessary to prevent deaths? We will never know because data are available to support a yes and a no. But the strategy of protracted lockdowns confused epidemiological data with Bigger Picture reasoning. That was a disaster.

Whether you supported the lockdowns or not, you should carefully weigh real data-driven versus data-drivel.

Quick takeaways for the road:

> *Insisting on "more data" runs the risk of behing left behind.*
>
> *Opportunities come from competitive intelligence quest-signals of things to come, not evidence things have already passed one over.*

> *Pushing for agility and more data-driven decisions are like asking a snail to run.*

> *Contrary to common misconception, accuracy is the enemy of strategic thinking. Being anal-retentive on spelling doesn't make one a writer. It just confirms one is anal-retentive.*

> *Extrapolation is not imagination, and assuming away surprises is not strategy.*

Chapter 7:
How Companies Inadvertently Sabotage Their Managers' Competitive Intelligence Quest (For Opportunities)

The proliferation of data platforms can be a boon for companies looking to improve operations. But, at the same time, it is detrimental to finding opportunities based on scarce early signals. What companies need to foster is the skill of *filtering* noise. Instead, inadvertently, companies discourage such filtering by frowning on the most effective human filter:

Skepticism.

Education, function, seniority, and position have nothing to do with the ability to go on a competitive intelligence quest for market insight. Still, one trait- born with or acquired – seems well correlated with filtering noise. Of course, correlation is not causality, and there are no Big Data to support this inference, but it makes sense. In a way, this is my *abductive* reasoning based on training thousands of managers on six continents[15].

After following hundreds of trainees' careers, I conclude that skepticism is a quintessential characteristic of a market-facing manager looking to identify early signs of changing power balance.

Skepticism is not a negative quality. Instead, it's the precursor to developing an alternative perspective; An alternative view is the bread and butter of opportunities. Here is how the logic goes:

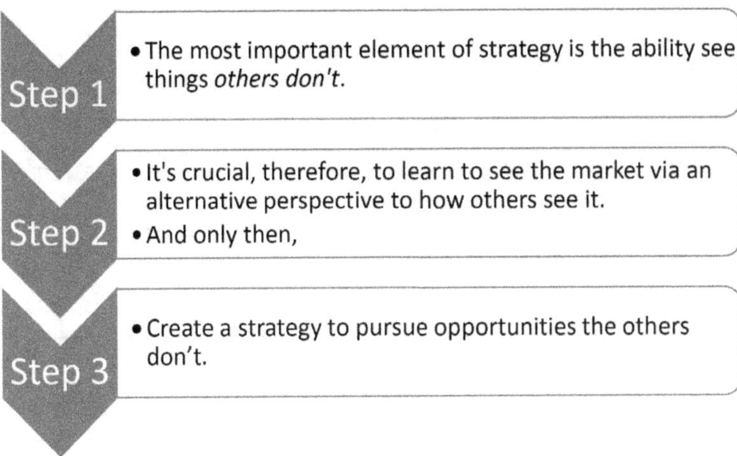

Skepticism is frowned upon in many companies. Counter-intuitive thinking is not encouraged in companies. "Keeping up with competitors" via imitation and benchmarking is more prevalent. But skepticism is crucial to reaching market insight.

An alternative perspective counters popular beliefs, a consensus of "experts," consulting companies' reports, Wall Street's valuation, and the instinctive desire to get more data. An alternative perspective is *not* the same as "Devil Advocate," which is an organizational unit or process deliberately set to argue a counterpoint to prevailing proposals. Being skeptical for the sake of being skeptical may be helpful, at times, to ward off careless taking on unnecessary risks, but it is not an effective mechanism to discover opportunities.

Seeing the world through the eyes of different parties and finding a way to take advantage of that deeper understanding is "magic." At the core of every startup, for example, are founders who believed customers were unhappy with existing solutions to their pains.

Most start-ups fail. Still, the skeptical perspective on what is already available drives entrepreneurs to offer an alternative. Likewise, incumbents- large companies competing against each other- can benefit from a bit of skepticism in their ranks instead of squashing it as "negativity."

Case in Point

In 2016, Walmart acquired Jet.com, an online shopping site, for a staggering $3.3 billion. In 2020, Walmart announced it is shutting down the site. A failure of that magnitude is not atypical with large companies, though often the acquisitions are dismantled quietly, absorbed, and dissipated without outsiders looking in. Examples include HP acquiring Palm Pilot, AOL acquiring ICQ, and Google acquiring Waze. In the case of Walmart, the failure was a tree falling in a forest full of observers.

What went wrong with Jet.com[16]?

Nothing. Yes, it sucked up cash at a terrific rate, incurred significant losses for Walmart, and created severe tensions between Marc Lore, its founder, and Walmart's US CEO, Greg Foran. But the primary failure was related to the original reason for the acquisition: to close the gap between Walmart's online commerce and Amazon.

Post all Walmart's accumulated investments in e-commerce and Jet.com, in 2019, Amazon had 38% of the online retail, and Walmart had...4%.

The Skeptical perspective on the travails with Jet.com is not hard to come by. In 2019, Amazon had 119 fulfillment centers, Walmart had 20. Walmart had 220,000 products online, and Amazon had 10 million. Come on, this was just an unfair fight. To even have a chance at catching up, Walmart needed considerable investments in warehouses and logistics and a willingness to cut down substantially on the returns to its investors. That conflicted with its need to invest in the stores and keep its lower prices. Any competition analyst with a brain could have predicted that strategy won't work in a consistently profitable company. Finally, Jet.com competed with Walmart.com. Does that make sense to anyone?

In 2020, Walmart folded Jet.com into Walmart.com. Marc Lori was made head of all e-Commerce[17]. Walmart could have done that four years ago. Walmart's e-commerce is growing (though presumed not to be profitable yet). Walmart has no choice but to jump on the e-Commerce wagon, which it sees as significant in the future of all retail. It also has no chance of catching up to Amazon.

For Walmart, this is a case of 'damn if you do and damn if you don't' and catering to the perspective of Wall Street instead of being strategically skeptical.

Alas, we tend to turn off our skepticism when successful people are involved. Instead, we should turn our doubt *up* because the glitter just adds to the noise.

A glance at CB Insights, a database documenting technology startups and trends, reveals a fascinating list of the biggest failures of all time.[18] So instead of going through all 208 companies, let's picked one: Quibi.

The list of backers - Goldman Sacks, JP Morgan, NBC Universal (part of Comcast)- is akin to the list of English Royals with a direct line to inherit the crown. The list of executives is even more impressive: founder Jeffrey Katzenberg and Chief Executive Meg Whitman. What can go wrong?

Quibi offered a revolutionary idea, content in short (5-10 min) chapters formatted for the cell phone screen with the biggest names in Hollywood behind these. It received $1.75 billion in funding. The problem was Tik-Tok, and YouTube offered it already for free. The second problem was one couldn't share it with friends. The third problem was the content was bad.

Quibi shut down six months after it launched due to low demand, stiff competition (accounting for low demand), and clunky technology. As USA Today said, "No one could possibly have seen this turn of events, except, you know, everyone who wasn't involved in the creation of Quibi itself.[19]"

Quick takeaways for the road:

> *The opposite of alternative perspective is competitive convergence via imitation and benchmarking.*

> *We tend to turn off our skepticism when successful people are involved. Instead, we should turn our skepticism up because the glitter just adds to the noise.*

Chapter 8: Organizational Culture as the Scapegoat?

In diagnosing obstacles to competitive intelligence-seeking behavior, outside experts and insiders often mention culture as one of the main culprits. However, a deeper dive into this generalized claim suggests that common claims of complacent management, slow to act, or risk-averse to the extreme may not be the specific hindrance to competitive intelligence quests as much as a more basic corporate characteristic: The demand for "facts."

It is symptomatic of many corporate presentations that managers often revert to "fluff" whenever they don't have the logic. Fluff can be multiple "bullet points" presented as separate facts but repeating an argument or a pile of facts that in total do not add to the conclusion drawn. For managers, it's a survival instinct in large companies.

In our book, *The NEW Employee Manual- A No-Holds-Barred Look at Corporate Life* (Entreprenerd Press, 2019), my co-author, Mark Chussil, a leading authority on strategy simulations, and I take a close look at fluff. Top executives typically have no patience for *qualitative* fluff. Their fluff is of a different kind- fictitious ROI and cash flow models and P&L "sensitivity analysis" provided by their external consulting firms at the drop of a hat (or a Monte Carlo simulation engine).

So why do managers keep up the fluff? They say, simply: "Culture."

Culture is an easy scapegoat when things go wrong, and it is an easy "explanation" for ineffective behaviors.

Then there is the famous cliché of "Culture eats strategy for breakfast." It's part of this fluff because there is no such animal as "culture" divorced from strategy itself. On the contrary, an organization's strategy reflects its culture, which in turn is shaped by its strategy. So how can culture eat strategy? It's like a snake eating its own tail.

Culture eats strategy for breakfast suggests that the best strategies fail because culture prevented their successful *implementation*. 21% of the CEOs in the Economist/PMI survey quoted earlier cite it as a reason for strategic failure.

The reality, as presented by that same survey, is quite different. Let me reproduce Figure 2 here:

None of the above is the fault of some mythical "culture." Yes, organizations do become arrogant and complacent at times, but the entire managerial cadre does not. Instead, individual managers still identify opportunities to advance their company's goals.

Recall Figure 3:

- Competitor offerings — 69%
- Changes in customer needs — 66%
- New entrants — 65%
- Current customer needs — 64%
- Current competitor strategies — 63%
- Likely changes in competitor behavior — 63%

The problem is that instead of fostering competitive intelligence quest for opportunities, management tasks the various functions and external agencies with *monitoring* the environment. They do it faithfully. They just don't produce competitive intelligence because the culture demands data, not speculations. So, they pile on data, report every competitor's moves, product announcements, market statistics, and so on. When executives demand the reporting of "facts," market insight is obstructed.

It is clear from the figures above that strategy failure precedes implementation failure. When the strategy designers are surprised by a grocery list of developments in the market, strategy at the outset was good only in the executives' eyes as they assumed the infamous "ceteris paribus" (All Else Equal). Overlooking the impact of third parties on outcomes is common among powerful people.

Early opportunities have very few facts to support them. The "secret" of true competitive intelligence, separated by a gulf from data/information, is in the interpretation of few facts as signals for things to come. Facts don't have intrinsic value, so more facts are not better facts. Nowhere is this more evident than in the so-called market "analysis" industry.

Companies waste millions on unnecessary "research"

Market reports help monitor the execution of existing strategies. They can point, in retrospect, when things haven't worked as expected. Market research reports often put a disclaimer at the outset, saying it is their *interpretation* of publicly available information. Yet too many reports are filled to the brim with tables and charts and numbers representing the past, not an insightful interpretation signaling things to come early on.

What does management do with thousands of pages of facts from a rearview mirror?

Typically- very little.

What do salespeople do with "battle cards" that are continually updated by Artificial Intelligence?

Very little. Salespeople have little patience for facts.

What do marketers do with facts from technology bolstered "news" aggregators?

They read them carefully, find consolation in outcomes they like, become disappointed in undesirable consequences, then move on. At times they may use a few facts to create bullet points fluff for their next presentation.

The organization's strategy doesn't change with facts; the sales tactics don't change with facts; You know the bulk of this noise as GTK (good to Know). It's equivalent to background cosmic hum. Management likes being "fully informed."

A fully informed management is not synonymous with better informed. Often, it's just a symptom of insecurity of FOMO (Fear of Missing Out) or FOMU (Fear of Messing Up). It is not that different than our teenage kids checking their feed every few minutes.

I am not claiming all market reports are useless, as management does need to keep an eye on what is happening. But the main problem is that one can never be "fully informed" about the future, and management "kills" the competitive intelligence-seeking behaviors of its own market-facing managers by insisting on reporting facts. There should be a separate channel for competitive intelligence, but often there isn't.

How to escape JTFP?

One and a half minutes into reading a so-called intelligence document or watching a PowerPoint presentation is enough to accurately sense corporate culture regarding JTFP: "Just the facts, please." In some companies, management demands volumes of data. The result is that the managers produce volumes of data. But even in such cultures, competitive intelligence-seeking managers playing the game by making volumes of noise from the most expensive resources flash out the nuggets of real value, which are neither facts nor typically from a vendor. They do it by inserting comments, implications, and at times, recommendations into a routine report. Management often ignores these, and nasty VPs may send an email asking "JTFP," but persistence can pay in the long run. Cato the Elder, a Roman senator, was famously ending each of his speeches regardless of the topic with a call to destroy Carthage. Eventually, his call was heeded.

Facts are empty calories. Intelligence is the diet. Pay for the former, get a heart attack. Look for the latter, get healthy.

CAGR on a toast

A popular feature of market analysis by reputable agencies includes CAGR -projections of compounded average growth rate per segment. But, alas, the nature of statistical models used to forecast CAGR means that by the time these vendors signal "hot" areas for growth, it is too late to make any real return there, as all the large companies competitively converge on it.

Managers alert to signs of change in their market do not produce CAGR. There is a clear distinction between a forecast and prediction. The latter is based on early signals, intuition, personal sense of where things move, idiosyncratic contact with other players, and entrepreneurial alertness long before analytics call out trends. Predictions of market change do not pretend to be accurate, just insightful. Opportunities propose options for management to shape the market before it becomes shaped by others.

Don't blame ambiguous culture. Blame the specific insistence on "facts."

Quick takeaways for the road:

> *Facts don't have intrinsic value, so more facts are not better facts.*

> *Overwhelming share of spending on market data/information by companies - millions and millions of dollars - is driven by FOMO or its cousin, FOMU.*

> *Facts are empty calories. Intelligence is the diet. Rely on the former, get a heart attack. Look for the latter, get healthy.*

> *The main value of competitive intelligence is enabling companies to shape the market before others shape it for them.*

Chapter 9:
The Risk of Focusing on Risks

Among other corporate practices that hinder the quest for opportunities using competitive intelligence, one stands out: Executive attention to risks.

It is a well-known "secret" among corporate competitive intelligence practitioners to capture management attention by mentioning "disruption" and competitive risks. This practice, however, can turn against opportunity identification. The reason is simple: business is not national security. Risks are hardly ever about an imminent attack. Imminent attacks may occur in cyberspace, but data security is not competitive intelligence.

Counterintelligence, threat identification, and other terms don't belong in competitive intelligence, which this book defines as market insight about competitive edge. These risks are in the domain of security—two different animals. Companies might as well place cafeteria food safety in there too.

Proponents of this confusion pose the same line of reasoning that says business war games are about wars. The terminology may be convenient in connoting the nature of considering *other players'* perspectives in pressure-testing strategy, but business is not war by any stretch of the imagination. Those who think business is war lack imagination or lack judgment.

The main focus of competitive intelligence-seeking behaviors of market-facing managers should be on finding opportunities for an edge. This subconscious alertness to opportunities runs along with the daily grind of managers' conscious tasks that involve a lot of what is known as "stick fetching." Stick fetching is the task of finding facts and figures to plug into the routine reports and documents submitted and distributed in a company. Stick fetching involves many "warnings" about competitive "threats," but few of those are significant compared to finding growth opportunities. The din of stick fetching is so loud in a typical company that many managers forget that competing means alertness to opportunities.

Alertness to opportunities- the relentless, subconscious scanning for an edge- is essential for functions such as strategic planning, marketing, business development, sales, and technology scouting. Gaining management attention might be easier using fear, and managers might be inclined to report risks out of FOMU, but heeding off threats does not necessarily lead to growth. Identifying specific options for pursuing opportunities does.

Excessive focus on reporting risks has some unintended consequences; it may turn customers off like other repeated behavior. Once customers stop listening, it is hard to regain their attention.

Dystopian future

During the Covid epidemic, Netflix found a very profitable niche in producing and streaming dystopian movies and series. Barren landscape, burning cars on bridges, and the collapse of civilization due to mysterious virus was one theme. Another common theme was an AI-backed totalitarian ruler or aliens controlling a slave society.

I've watched maybe 13 of those movies in the past year, and they keep coming. I am now dystopian-out. I can't even look at another smoky bridge or tyrant's face. Why do I get so many of them? Because Netflix's algorithm sees my preference and ceases on it and in the "recommended for you" section provides me with more of the same. But what if one likes variety?

Netflix is not alone. On LinkedIn, clicking "like" on posts generates similar topics to the exclusion of others. Algorithms tend to congregate us in groups of "insiders" and "outsiders." There is a similar tendency for executives to receive lots of warnings about competitive risks. Management tires of the same bad news bearer crying "wolf." They just stop listening.

If done well, risk mitigation is an integral part of intelligence-seeking behavior, but it can't be the only or even the main message. Opportunities are way more intriguing to management. Both risks and opportunities emerge from *changes* in industry structure. For example, VW's management perspective on the lack of competition in the US for diesel engines while European governments welcome the alternative to gasoline was seen as an opportunity for growth. It was a false opportunity- the engineering solution for very stringent emission controls in the US was not available, but opportunity is always in the user's eye. It doesn't have to be real or correct.

Opportunities are much more difficult to spot and deliver, but they are like a romantic comedy popping up on my Netflix "you may like this too" list- full of promise and pink hope.

The analogy with Netflix algorithms is apt: algorithms are overkill in the search for opportunities. They can serve a limited purpose of keeping users "updated" for no reason other than closely monitoring traffic in their space, but they have little use in generating new perspectives. Though it seems every week another A/I-driven data "platform" pops up, these platforms are not a panacea for the most critical role of the intelligence quest. Instead, managers and analysts should expand their "search" to include areas unrelated to their industry or products. Insights are rare and valuable, and if A/I algorithms could find them, everyone will be on the same page instantly. But that isn't the case, is it?

I got my idea for the first war game methodology used in a commercial enterprise in the US back in 1982 when I read Orson Card's Ender series. If I used a data/research/news platform, it would have probably recommended War and Peace. If I subscribed to one of the multitudes of cyber threats services claiming they are in competitive intelligence, it would have identified a threat to national security from reading Ender's Game.

Quick takeaways for the road:

> *Counterintelligence, threat identification, and data security do not belong in competitive intelligence. They are a different animal altogether.*

> *Serendipity is a powerful source of insight in competing in any area. All you need is the habit of alertness to changes in the Big Picture operating in the background.*

Chapter 10:
Getting Management to Change Its Mind

The first step towards renewed growth advocated in this book is to actively encourage competitive intelligence-seeking behaviors of market-facing managers, salespeople, and professionals. To be consistent with Corporate terminology, I should abbreviate it to CISB for MS&P.

Why do managers use so many acronyms? The creation and communication of acronyms signify to top management that the speaker is not wasting time on trivial, well-known concepts.

But just because management cadre (especially junior to middle) is alert to opportunities and uses the correct number of acronyms doesn't mean the fight is over. Getting through to top management is always a struggle.

The art of persuading others is far from trivial. It is doubly challenging to impact executives who rarely think people outside their trusted circle have anything interesting to say. Even a young leader like Luke Skywalker didn't want to listen to old and wise Yoda, and if this reference is too obscure for you, you are the Z Generation.

The famous anecdote about how Andy Grove, Intel's legendary leader, decided to ditch its main cash driver- memory chips- tells of a presentation he'd seen from Harvard's Clayton Christensen about disruptions. This tale is typical of how leaders form their perspectives *and who gets to influence them.* Peers. Outside advisors. Investment bankers. Large customers. Inner circle (to a degree).

That is it. No one else is entering the shrine.

Rory Sutherland, Vice Chairman of Ogilvy Consultants in the UK, a marketing outfit, famously said, "[in corporate decision making] fear of regret, which drives individual decisions, gives way to fear of blame: a decision which is easy to defend, or one which delivers small but quantifiable incrementable improvements, will be preferred to one which overall is better for the health of the organization.[20]"

Gerd Gigerenzer, a famous psychologist, studying intuition in organizational settings, describes this behavior as Defensive Decision-Making. "As a result, much activity within workplaces is almost certainly arse-covering disguised as rigour[21]." And David Ogilvy said, "People are using statistics as a drunk uses a lamppost: for support rather than illumination."

How can a manager, even one skilled in competitive intelligence-seeking, hope to break into that club?

How one talks to management is closely related to the fact that having a market insight doesn't translate straight forward to changing management perspective.

"I wish we could say that"

The current thinking on cognition and learning posits an ingrained cognitive structure (schema) that controls the acquisition of new knowledge by directing attention. Facts and opinions that agree with the schema are added to memory. Those that contradict the schema (plural, schemata) will be more likely to be rejected or heard selectively. In other words, we see what we want to see, and if it doesn't fit our model of the world (schema), we may just ignore it. Nothing new here, except that schema is resistant to change. *Facts or logic don't always change a schema.* At times, the schema is so unrealistic it becomes pathological. That's when CBT (cognitive behavior therapy) presumably works (and if not, there is always bankruptcy court).

The concept of established schema explains two issues:

First, it demonstrates why practicing the Big Picture model in Chapter 3 is essential to create alertness. Ingraining a new framework of looking at the competitive arena directs attention to new opportunities.

Second, it explains why highlighting opportunities rather than risks have a better chance of getting through the schema. Management might see opportunities as less of a direct attack on their existing schema.

Both intelligence and economics share this in common: they direct our attention to understanding the schemata (core assumptions) of other parties *without emotional or value judgment.* Economics does it to arrive at macro predictions. Competitive intelligence does it to develop micro-predictions.

Similarly, in presenting market insight to top management, a manager must understand their audience's schemata. Surprisingly, in some large companies, that might be as difficult as assessing competitors' perspectives. A manager down in the belly of a massive beast like Amazon or Microsoft might have a hard time understanding their big bosses' concerns and interests. Their bosses don't share an update on their thinking very often with their managers, and whatever they do share gets distorted.

As a message from the bottom makes its way upstairs, in turn, it is filtered, massaged, and molded to fit what the silos and chain of command *believe* will interest the top.

At best, this is guesswork. At worse, it masks real insights.

In war games, I am often told, "We wish we could say what you say to management." External authorities have a higher probability of being heard than employees. There are self-evident things they can't say (while an outsider can) and things they should say that *have zero chance of getting through due to schema's difference.* How can a company overcome this obstacle to find growth opportunities?

The art of talking to management: truth or politics?

What middle management tells top management falls into one of three types of messages:

- It can be consistent with the top bosses' schemata about the competitive arena, but it is boring if it is too consistent. They already know it. It's what expected. It is deemed redundant. Many managers choose this route early on in their job, mostly out of fear of being wrong, and they are then forever relegated to the "uninteresting" category.
- It can be so far outside the bosses' schemata that they will reject it offhand. A central assumption in this book is that for better or worse (often worse), top management just doesn't see what lower ranks see. The Executive's schemata and the manager's schemata are pretty different, and it's not always possible or even desirable to reconcile

them. There are behavioral techniques to frame a pitch to attempt and overcome this gap without being thrown out of the room earlier than expected.

- Perhaps the best tactic is to walk the thin line of being within their schemata but outside it in at least one aspect. I.e., being somehow intriguing is way more important than being right or wrong (and undoubtedly more important than data dumps that are just more noise). So the first step is to try and understand management's schemata; see the world from their perspective, *judgment-free.* The second is to find an angle for an *opportunity,* not a threat, in *any* situation. Threat narrows management's attention, the opposite of allowing them to accept your schema. Not easy. Not trivial. Way more subtle and sophisticated than "just give them the facts."

For example, think about a panhandler on the street asking for money, with a dog by his side. Here are two options for what he writes on the piece of cardboard he lays on the wall:

Hungry, Need Help (expected in our schema about the homeless) or,

My Dog Needs Its Alcohol Too (within our schema but not entirely expected).

The question is not which message will push one to act (give the man some money), but which message would get more attention.

If an opportunity is widely expected, it's no longer an opportunity as everyone converges on it. So, by default, an opportunity must be somewhat outside what management expected and therefore grab their attention.

Not to belabor the analogy, management must first look at the cardboard on the wall. For that, we have behavioral economics.

Quick takeaways for the road:

> *Understanding without value-judging is the first step to seeing different perspectives in the market.*

> *Being intriguing is way more important than being accurate or even right in getting a point across.*

PART III:
What Can Companies do to Support Competitive Intelligence Quests?

Chapter 11:
What VW and Google Teach Us NOT to do

While it is relatively easy to assess culture by reading just one internal intelligence document (see Chapter 8), the reverse is not that simple. It is hard to honestly know how well intelligence-seeking behavior embeds in an organization by just looking at its culture. Despite the well-known "intelligence culture" concept proposed by some respected experts, I haven't found such an animal after working with world-leading companies for over two decades. It's like Winnie the Poo's mystical Heffalump.

Intelligence is in the eye of the user, not the beholder. Since the user is top management, and the beholders are thousands of frontline employees in market-facing functions, the attitude of the top towards opportunities can either foster intelligence seeking or squash it. Unfortunately, in most Western companies, this is idiosyncratic and depends on individual leadership as much as on competitive pressures in the industry.

No one can force managers to seek opportunities, but a company can encourage it in both formal and informal ways.

Rivalry and intelligence-seeking behavior

There are some famous rivalries in markets that typically generate competitive intelligence-seeking behaviors. The type of opportunities sought, though, may depend on the nature of the industry. For example, in some software segments, competitive edge is relatively short-lasting, so almost by default, the battle is fought at the sales force level using hand-to-hand combat over "customer relationships." Such contests foster tactical, short-sighted sales support. Strategic intelligence-seeking is left to the thin strata of top management level, with the (at times dubious) help of investment bankers proposing candidates for (at times questionable) acquisitions. Then comes a startup with a completely new approach to some service, and the big incumbents scramble to understand what happened. This wake-up call is not a "cultural" issue. It's economics at its best: protecting legacy assets (generating most of the cash flow) is a simple survival tactic for management for whom short-term results determine bonuses (with some wink, wink, gesture to amorphous long-term performance). No large organization can escape this internal conflict between legacy assets and new product/service areas, and this accounts for more legacies failing over time than "complacent cultures." The result in legacy-rich companies is that intelligence-seeking behavior by managers facing a competitive marketplace (known in economics as contested markets) is not driven by incentives to look at what is around the curve but what is coming at them at full speed. Can companies fight such instincts?

Retraining corporate culture?

Whatever we perceive as "company culture," is it possible to change it?

It is exceedingly easy to change culture, whatever the culture is. All that is needed is a Private Equity firm stepping in and culture changes in a hurry. Short of this brutal change, the idea of "transformation" is fodder for MBA classes and consultants. They all have good intentions and effective models, and in the end, very little changes.

Companies that changed drastically over the years are few and far between. For example, IBM went from hardware to software ("solution") company only after a brutal period in which it was under existential threat to its model.

Instead of changing the entire culture, which often seems more a slogan than reality, companies can simply restructure incentives to competitive intelligence-seeking behaviors.

What should companies do to create an intelligence-seeking "culture"?

Short of brutal shakeup that comes from a change in ownership, changing the way managers seek and use information about creating an edge is down to two issues:

1. Incentives
2. HR practices

Economists know that incentives induce behaviors. So part of the art of looking at the competitive arena from the perspective of the other players is that if you follow the incentives, you can, to *some degree*, predict behavior.

In 2015, VW, The German automaker, admitted publicly to installing software in its diesel engines since 2005 that sensed when the engine was being tested for pollution emission and slowed down its performance so that the results were close to 40 times lower than its emission on the road.

That was ingenious. At the outset, VW top executives blamed a few mid-level managers and engineers. Then as the scandal widens, a few of the same top executives were found to be lying (shocking!). A few were ousted. Later, a few went to jail. As late as 2019, a few are charged with financial fraud as they failed to inform shareholders of the seriousness of the scandal. It is hard to understand who among the leadership team remains, as VW's governing structure is a nightmare of German hierarchy and infantile roles for various stakeholders. But the real question was simple: *Why* cheat?

According to an article in Newsweek by Leah McGrath Goodman titled Why Volkswagen Cheated (12/15/15), one can trace the first incentive to government regulations. Not surprising, as all government regulations come with unintended consequences and a lot of fraud in trying to circumvent them. There is a reason why classical market economists condemn regulations as the least efficient way to improve outcomes.

In 2004, the US Environmental Protection Agency (EPA) raised the bar on how much pollution new cars in the U.S. would be permitted to discharge into the atmosphere. The move was not gradual- it was dramatic. But, unfortunately, it also presented an impossible engineering challenge to the world's automakers within a short time and limited budget. That was especially problematic to diesel-fueled cars, where the exhaust contains more nitrogen dioxide than gasoline-powered cars.

Diesel cars get better mileage and hold their long-term value better than most gasoline-burning vehicles. In their zeal to show progress against gas guzzlers, European governments encouraged the sale of diesel cars because they consume less fuel. The result of that incentive? More than 50 percent of vehicles sold in Europe were diesel. In the US, less than 5 percent. Ironically, the emission standards and tests in Europe were much less stringent.

There starts the chain of incentives: Cracking the US market was VW's top priority since its bosses were heavily incentivized to become the world's *number one* automaker, beating Toyota. The scope for growth was immense.

Incentive schemes in the German automaker had several effects on behavior. First, its hierarchical, autocratic German nature severely discouraged dissent and debate. The threat of losing one job if management was displeased with one's performance was a great incentive to find shortcuts and avoid making trouble. As Newsweek's quote those familiar with VW culture, "at Volkswagen, the management might say, 'Please think again on that, and if you don't find a solution, we may need to find another engineer.'"

But that's just the beginning of tracing behavior to incentives. Companies are not democracies; VW wasn't the only company where the pressure to perform resulted in undesired behaviors. Think Wells Fargo in the US. Sure, German autocracy may be infamous for demanding compliance, but that is not enough. You have to offer positive reinforcement as well.

At VW, employees may have remained quiet about the emissions-cheating issue because it paid off. The company has an exceedingly generous bonus system, unlike any other automaker. Volkswagen pays bonuses for individual performance, company performance, and *team performance*, creating significant pressure for consensus.

Naturally, following the scandal and the coverup, interested parties paid lip service to the need to change the climate in which problems are hidden and make it "possible and permissible to argue with your superior about the best way to go."

Anyone believing this will happen, please raise your hand. There is a 1000 Euros bonus if you raise your hand.

Interestingly, Volkswagen's Asian rivals Mazda, Honda, Nissan, and Hyundai canceled their plans to offer diesel engines in the US. Of course, no one will claim that Asian cultures are more open to dissent, but the incentive to cheat – especially at the top- may be smaller.

One thing is clear: Incentives do work. Always. No matter if you are a socialist, communist, capitalist, or paganist. *Always.*

What type of incentives will foster intelligence-seeking behaviors?

There are no golden rules nor "winning formulae" for that. Intelligence seeking depends on whom the company recruits. It also depends on how much employees and managers are encouraged to "think big." Window dressing speeches won't do it.

One area where incentives can work in American companies is *individual* recognition, not team bonuses, in designing the internal information flows resulting in gaining an edge (i.e., developing market insights that a company uses to gain a competitive advantage.) The American cultural focus on merit and individual exceptionalism has produced the world's most robust economy by far. The future might belong to China's obedient and carefully monitored and controlled workforce, but history, including the fall of Japan's economy, suggests otherwise. On the other hand, the demise of exceptionalism for more "equity" may end the great American experiment in competing (and winning). There should be a way to balance the two.

Human Resource Management and the destruction of intelligence seeking

The Woke culture rising in the US might have had some good intentions to be more sensitive to human sensitivities. Enforced by institutional bullying via regulations-favoring HR departments, however, discouraged individual's intelligence seeking tendencies. To prioritize not offending anyone is wrong. Offending is not, should not, be a capital crime in a free society or growth-seeking company.

It takes a great deal of integrity for scholars to stand up to the damaging extreme Woke norms affecting competitiveness in American corporations. Unfortunately, only a few scholars have integrity in US academia where tenure depends on peers' approval (*incentives work* principle). This book will not change Woke's destructive path. The only thing that will stop it from destroying every American company is when China takes over American Human Resource departments and teach them how to behave. Ironically, offensive behavior is typical in Chinese management directed from senior to junior staff, and the only offense punishable by torture and potential disappearance is against the CCP.

To see how Woke norms affect the ability to compete, one needs to look no further than the clash between startups' culture and the behemoths who acquire them.

Can a giant behemoth and a small startup live happily together? Can a massive behemoth keep the startup spirit? Can a giant behemoth even feel when it sits on and squashes the startup? Anecdotal evidence suggests that the answer is a resounding no[22]. Of course, it is hard to collect more than anecdotal evidence since most acquiring giants will never admit to a resounding failure of the acquisition. But insiders know the real stories.

The startup nation of Israel is the place of more startups per capita than anywhere else in the world. It provides clues to the answer to keeping the competitive intelligence-seeking initiatives alive in a big company's environment.

In the past decade alone, Israeli high-tech startups made 1,210 exits for 111 billion dollars. That's more than the GNP of Latvia, Bolivia and Uganda combined. Tel Aviv is one of the best cities in the world to create a startup (1 per 100 residents) if you can find parking.

The experience of some of these startup icons hasn't always been encouraging for coexistence with the large acquiring companies. Israeli culture is blunt, direct, and some say aggressive. Sensitivity is not precisely the hallmark. Diversity and Woke slogans aren't common at all. Perhaps because Israel never had a moment of peace, it escaped the worse of Woke mentality. It didn't see the existential threat coming from verbal offense to others but from the desire of others to obliterate the Jewish state. So what happens when a brazen Israeli entrepreneur meets US Woke culture? See below.

Case in Point

Are you familiar with Elton John's song, Benny and the Jets? Sing it but use Google and the Waze instead. It could have been an excellent name for a rock band if it weren't a sad saga.

In 2013, Google acquired an Israeli startup called Waze for close to a billion dollars. In 2020, the founder, Noam Bardin, resigned from Google. When asked how come he left after seven years, he replied, the question is how come I lasted that long.

In a damning post[23] on Paygo media, itself a startup, Mr. Bardin described Google's culture as an ossified nightmare. The gist? "An ever-increasing percent of our time went to non-user value creation tasks, and that changes the DNA of the company quickly, from customer-focused to corporate guidelines focused."

This story is the ever typical one. When the beast buys the beauty, the beast pushes the customer to the end of the list. Thus, what has been the startup's beloved, cherished, true focus of attention becomes a beasts' regurgitated slogan, "the customer is our focus."

No, it's not. Have you ever tried to reach Google's customer service? How about Facebook?

The cultural divide between a startup's attention to its customers and a behemoth's focus is unbridgeable, so when the behemoth acquires the startup, it inevitably destroys its focus. Reading Waze's Bardin's damning description of Google's culture and its "prized" employees, one gets the feeling that Google is nearing the end of its reign. Those dismissing such dire prediction as impossible, remember a company called Zeppelin, the once ruler of the skies, Pride of Germany. The Hindenburg was Zeppelin's flagship product. Just google it.

Or rather, DuckDuckGo it.

The F... word as a symbol of decline

The generalization of "culture eats strategy for breakfast" is incorrect. Instead, it is a specific large company's culture that eats strategy and gets heartburn. To recognize it, you don't need a lot of competitive intelligence; you just need to watch the language used by executives.

Mr. Bardin's hilarious recollection of his numerous appearances in Google's internal forums tells all. He was a popular speaker – a successful entrepreneur who created a truly unique product. Waze changed the world of navigation and avoiding police traps for speeding, nothing short of monumental progress. But being an Israeli and an entrepreneur, he was politically incorrect. He used the F word.

The F word (as in Fuck, not Finance) connotes passion. Passion fuels intelligence-seeking in search for insights. Passion motivates System 1. Passion directs focus for System 2. Passion is everything in competing.

One uses the F word to motivate, arouse passion, show commitment to an idea, and contempt towards stupidity (and occasionally, competitors). That didn't go well with Google's PC police. Correction: it didn't go well with some in the crowd. The crowd overall loved Noam, but the sensitive souls, PPOs (professionally and perennially offended) small minority complained to HR...

When HR runs companies, that is the first sign of decay. Once politically correct culture takes over, the tyranny of the Woke signals the end of the entrepreneurial, intelligence-seeking spirit. In large companies like Google, it signals the beginning of the end. My prediction: Google is dying; just wait for its bloated corpse to wash to the shore. It's not going to be pretty. The demise of Sears and General Electric wasn't.

It is not very surprising that some large companies and startups can't mesh. Nvidia bought Mellanox, another Israeli startup, for $7 billion in 2019. The founder, Eyal Waldman, didn't last even two full years. He left recently saying, I don't like being number 2 in any company.

Some readers and critiques of this perspective would argue that one can be passionate about competing without resorting to offensive language. This is a fundamental misunderstanding of the incentives for individual initiatives. It reflects the naïve belief that one can have the cake and eat it too. The idea that one can (and should) regulate, moderate, dictate the expression of passion and that a regulated, moderated, restrained passion is better has no empirical support. It is very similar to the idea that "open office" design encourages communication. The evidence points the other way.

The unadulterated passion for competing makes one's mind ready to see an opportunity. Unadulterated doesn't mean unethical, inhuman, or horribly greedy. It doesn't mean creating a hostile environment or harassing women, but it does mean being free to express strong emotions through words, including the occasional curse.

The surest way to kill the passion for competing in employees is to set the HR on them. Talent then goes on to create startups that we all need more than we need their old employers. Schumpeter, the famous economist, hailed it as *creative destruction*.

Careless Woke can be just the reverse: the destruction of the creative.

A company can't force competitive intelligence-seeking behaviors. It is sometimes easier just to pause and devise policies that *do not interfere* in individuals' quests. That requires courage and tolerance without sacrificing a safe working environment. An understanding that passion is not synonymous with abusive behavior is paramount. When recruiting talent is the number one issue for companies, restrictive HR is not an asset[24].

Quick takeaways for the road:

Legacy-rich companies foster intelligence seeking driven by incentives to look not at what is around the curve, but what is coming at them at full speed.

"Dear Abby: It offends me when people say being offensive is offending. What should I do?"

Offender

Unfettered capitalism fosters creative destruction, as new companies displace old ones. Woke norms foster destruction of creative as organizational regulation of passion ensures creatives leave for better companies.

Best advice to leaders looking to foster competitive intelligence seeking behaviors: It is easier to just pause and devise policies that do not interfere in individuals' quests.

Chapter 12:
The Sin of Pigeonholing

The concept of competitive intelligence-as-skill strongly supports the idea that competitive intelligence is not just a dedicated information function but a distributed skill for all market-facing managers. Market insight forming from aggregating individual alertness suggests the need for careful handling of the *source* of the insights.

Within corporate confines, alertness to opportunities is institutionalized in specific functions- the M&A department is a classic one. But this book advocates a broader net since opportunities are not confined to a few experts in a particular department. That designation defeats the notion of "voice of the market."

When I first ran our Foundation of Competition Analyst workshop, I didn't aim it at archivists, researchers, or information practitioners such as librarians. My bias suggested that these are less business-oriented and therefore less likely to notice an early signal of change in market structures.

Then one of the participants was a librarian. Librarians are by design archivists – store and retrieve information on demand - and are not supposed to have an opinion on the demand *or* the information.

But that is wrong. Some librarians are natural intelligence analysts and have a fresh perspective on the information, and one must ask: Can a leopard change its spots? (a biblical reference, Jeremiah 13).

The question is wrong. Of course, a leopard can change its spots! All it takes is a bit of photoshop. The problem is, would the bosses see them as a kitten?

Curiosity and non-linear thinking do not have to be confined to M&A functions (see Chapter 4). Grasping the big picture has little to do with rank, title, gender, childhood experience, or educational background[25]. Some of the most strategic thinkers have degrees in French Literature or Divinity Studies (actual data). But the issue is pigeonholing. And it adversely affects businesses' ability to benefit from market insights.

The damage of pigeonholing

Pigeonholing refers to the phenomenon of assessing someone's value according to her task/function, not her contribution. Corporate Pigeonholing is one bias not often discussed when news items mention widespread cognitive biases such as framing or anchoring or diversity and inclusion. We all pigeonhole almost instinctively.

The more common pigeonholing comes from companies relying heavily on specialized knowledge, such as high-tech environment or Pharma. In these environments, perspectives not backed by credentials as an engineer, or computer scientist, or life science expert get *automatically* discounted. Or, more accurately, pigeonholed to the area that person is assigned.

For example, "You may understand marketing, but this is technical." Or, "You may be good at information searches, but this is business."

To a degree, this is justified. There are technical areas (from accounting to legal to operations) where specific knowledge is a prerequisite for meaningful contribution. But that is not the case in one critical area: Strategy.

To a degree, information practitioners (such as corporate librarians or research managers) contribute to their own pigeonholing by hiding behind sending facts and doing background "research." So they shouldn't be surprised if later no one takes their attempts at competitive insight seriously. But when a librarian is smarter than those requesting the information, not listening to her can be a mistake.

Remember this simple principle behind a wide net of alertness to opportunities: What management sees from its upper floor isn't the same as what others see from the street.

Is there a "cure" to pigeonholing?

In some industries heavily dependent on specialized expertise as its main product, there is no cure. Many law firms' partners, for example, treat anyone who is not a lawyer as a service provider, not an equal partner to strategic discussions about opportunities. That includes their own marketing people.

Investment bankers treat back-office operations as a *backward* office. A large financial institution's CEO will likely treat a "stick fetcher" (employee he asks to provide some data for a random question without context or elaboration) as a stick fetcher even if she brought him a whole tree. While many firms today jump on the diversity wagon, the cultural change from pigeonholing at consulting, legal, financial companies, and big Fortune 500 behemoths must be way more radical to allow the diversity of *perspectives.*

One can see the Big Picture from a cubicle at the end of the room and be blind to it from the Board Room at the top of the office tower. Therefore, companies looking to maximize growth should rethink pigeonholing.

Quick takeaways for the road:

If you are "pigeonholed", there is still a hole there. Peek out.

PART IV:
Getting a Buy-in

Chapter 13:
Modern-day Machiavelli

The first step to discovering growth opportunities is for companies to create, sustain and foster individual quests for competitive intelligence.

The second step, which is as important, is to listen to them.

Niccolò Machiavelli, the Italian philosopher and diplomat, is best known for *The Prince,* published in 1523. The modern-day connotation of Machiavellian behavior is achieving one's goals via means of unsavory manipulations.

While many see Machiavellianism as unfavorable, it is so prevalent in political circles and corporate halls that using it to get management attention should be the norm, not the maligned exception. The modern-day manipulation experienced by all of us via marketing and social media has come to be expected and *accepted.*

Using Machiavellian techniques to change management's perspective entails utilizing the art and science of behavioral economics.

A relatively recent addition to classical economic principles, behavioral economics aims to explain choices, not just formally describe their consequences. Thus, while classical economics is based on praxeology- the theory of human action- behavioral economics is based on behavioral science- the theory of human choice. The behavioral economic discipline has acquired significant followings among economists and political scientists. The most famous work in behavioral economics came from two Israeli psychologists, Amos Tversky and Daniel Kahneman (the latter won the Noble Prize in economics for his work). Their focus, via a series of experiments, was on human error-collectively termed heuristics or cognitive biases - making formal rational judgment difficult.

The most sophisticated manipulation scheme at your fingertips

No one likes to be manipulated, yet the most sophisticated, "enlightened" governments in the world created what has become known as Nudge Departments to manipulate behavior on a massive scale. This is not a fake Russian conspiracy. This is the real story of two academics, Richard Thaler and Cass Sunstein, who in 2008 wrote a fun book called Nudge. Thaler later won the Noble for his work.

Nudging is also the most potent weapon middle managers could possess, legitimately, if they just understood how to use it for changing executives' perspectives.

The changing modus operandi of intelligence sums it all up

The Original Sin, not the catholic one but the Church of Competitive Intelligence, has been to posit competitive intelligence as focused on collecting (competitor) information. The early pioneers of the corporate intelligence model came from the military/government doctrine of intelligence, so they transferred the model to business. This "transference" syndrome created the modus operandi for the development of competitive intelligence that I will sum up as:

"Collect, then tell it straight."

Yes, it rhymes. But it also didn't work, as this modus operandi quickly ran into specific cognitive biases at the top. So instead, what we got was:

"If we like what we hear, you have a career."

The notion that competitive intelligence's principal value is in confirming top executives' preconceived market schemata – except for the rare occasions of surprises- is not hard to understand. In recent years, though, as organizations turned more towards a search for dwindling growth opportunities, taking advantage of the competitive intelligence available inside their own ranks must change the focus. Following the Covid epidemic, a very different modus operandi is rising to prominence. To make it memorable, let's sum it up as: *The Intelligence art means deliver it smart.*

We are never biased; everyone else is.

While top management might be *in theory* interested in opportunities discovered by managers in the field, the idea that middle managers can just send competitive intelligence upstairs and wait for a call just doesn't work. It might have been a reasonable approach before US companies formally adopted competitive intelligence (in the late 80s). Or, maybe it was appropriate right after the earth was formless and void and darkness was upon the face of the deep. At that time, when a small group of early entrepreneurs started a journey to popularize competitive intelligence activities, companies were enthusiastically claiming their people were the best source of competitive intelligence. Then gradually, management stopped listening.

The reasons why top management stopped listening were varied, but they always followed the second economic principle: Incentives did work. If an opportunity turns out to be an illusion, but a famous investment banker partner or a major consulting firm's partner offered it, top management had an excuse for its institutional investors- we followed the advice of the best people in the field. If they could add Gartner to the mix, they were totally safe. That's what Gigerenzer and Sutherland call Defensive Decision Making (see Chapter 10).

Getting management to listen to its own people is far more complicated than inspirational speakers admit. Contrary to PR messaging, leading companies do *not* focus on customers and do not listen to managers in the trenches. This is just reality. You can believe the PR, read the media interviews, and swallow the inspirational quotes from the top brass whole. Still, as you are not an insider, you are digesting fake news fed to you, ironically, via behavioral manipulation such as Framing.

It's the same reason guys on Tinder take photos of themselves with dogs. Poor dogs, after the shot, the guys just give them back to the pound or their exes.

Instead of waiting for Godot (a famous play by Samuel Beckett) or top management to pay attention, market-facing managers, salespeople, and professionals should turn to the Machiavellian art of using cognitive biases. Yes, *using*.

When thinking about cognitive biases, most people tend to look for how to overcome them, which is a total waste of time; One never gets rid of one's biases. Psychotherapists have a famous line, being aware of issues is the first step to recovery. The reality, however, is that the first step is typically the last as well. Otherwise, psychotherapy would last all of three meetings.

Instead of fighting one's own relatively innocuous biases, here are several practical ways to turn *management's* biases *into openness to opportunities* and gain attention to competitive intelligence.

The journey to being an honest Machiavellian

Most business books' authors don't talk much about their past. They focus on the tools and advice. But the tools and advice, in this case, are firmly rooted in my personal journey before becoming a competitive intelligence "guru."

Before I founded the Academy and was no longer a police detective, I "served" 18 years in a business school. My field was economics and later strategy (strategy is rooted in the economics of industries), but my research interest was behavioral economics. I organized the first conference on behavioral economics ever convened back in the early 80s; I brought Daniel Kahneman, Richard Thaler, and Thomas Schilling as speakers. All these fine gentlemen won Noble Prize in economics later. Mine was lost in the mail from Sweden, so I transferred my limited talent to competitive intelligence training.

Just 30 years later, the concept of cognitive biases has become mainstream. It exploded, as expected, first into the popular business publications like Harvard Business Review, then into the Chronic Consulting firms and Ted talks. All applications of the concept, without exception, focused on advice to Leaders on how to prevent, avoid and overcome their biases, to become better leaders, happier people, admired clear-eyed icons who keep hiring these consultants.

No one focused on the real problem: How can an analyst or a manager, several levels down at the belly of the beast, supposed to overcome top executives' biases? With 15 minutes a quarter (if lucky) in front of the Leaders with a vast differential in power and status, are middle managers going to lift the veil off the eyes of the Ones with the Reserved Parking Spaces? Who are we *kidding?*

Getting management to pay attention is the just first step. The next step is changing management's perspective. Both have a higher probability of occurrence if the manager on a competitive intelligence quest uses Nudge Theory.

Nudge theory at work

Years after his stellar presentation at my conference, Richard Thaler introduced the famous Nudge theory. When governments want to encourage (what they consider) desirable behavior of the clueless masses– such as saving for retirement - they make employees automatically enrolled in pension contribution schemes and add an "opt-out" option. This auto-enrollment scheme works like a charm. This simple manipulation of *how information is presented* is scarily powerful in managing the populace. Governments in Australia, France, Spain, Singapore, UK, and, yes, the US adopted it quickly and wholeheartedly.

Underlying the Nudge model is a clear understanding of people's biases (shortcuts that influence decisions). Using it to turn data into market insight that changes management assumptions requires identifying the *most likely* biases at the top; Not all biases are equal. Then, if a manager tailors the delivery to take advantage of those biases while the audience makes biased judgments subconsciously, biases are an unexpected gift; experts call this manipulation "choice/option architecture."

Here is an example.

Research documents a "cognitive rigidity" phenomenon in many successful companies whereby top management is reluctant to change proven formulae. It manifests itself in several famous heuristics being present when top management makes decisions, including confirmation bias, attitude polarization, and framing effect. These heuristics predict– *to a degree-* the openness of executives to a specific type of ideas. Understanding how cognitive rigidity works allows managers and analysts to avoid being shot down quickly. That is a benefit since the longer managers engage in a productive dialogue with the top executives, the higher the probability of affecting their thinking. Remember the motto, "If we like what we hear, you have a career"? There is empirical evidence that engaging management in a dialogue about the Big Picture enhances the prospects of a successful career.

I know what you are thinking- this is manipulative and wrong. But is it?

Supporters of nudge manipulation claim it is for the social good and benefit of everyone. If readers understand competitive intelligence (i.e., can distinguish between mere information and an option to pursue opportunity), one can absolutely make similar claims. Getting management to listen favorably to its people when it comes to spotting growth opportunities can improve outcomes for both the manager and the company.

Quick takeaways for the road:

"The intelligence art means deliver it smart."

Instead of trying to eradicate innocuous middle managers' biases, use cognitive biases to get a buy-in. Yes, be Machiavellian.

Behavioral economic tools are used to point out blinders and judgmental errors. What happens if we turn the table on that?

Choice architecture can be used to change management perspectives, just as it is used by governments to change people's choices.

The longer one engages management in a dialogue, the higher the probability of an impact.

Chapter 14:
Framing a Message

The essence of reporting a potential opportunity for (profitable) edge to management is to deliver a *message*. Sometimes it is a message they want to hear and sometimes, it's not. The question of how to make it palatable is critical. Just reporting on what's happening is journalism. A perspective is an employee's **value add**.

Framing a perspective, though, is one cognitive bias managers should learn to exploit. The example below does not intend to take sides in the politicized issue of alternative energy sources and climate change. Instead, it is a lesson delivered by NY Times reporters on how to frame a message. Whether you are on the conservative or progressive side of the debate is utterly immaterial.

<table>
<tr><td>

Case in Point

The unprecedented storm that froze the Texas electric grid in February of 2021 hasn't even dried on paper – let alone on the solar panels- before the NY Times explained what caused it.

When newspaper publishers delivered newspapers to the front door every morning, editors could keep relatively neutral reporting standards since subscribers will not bother canceling the entire subscription due to an article they didn't like. These days, when newspapers have paywalls- and measuring precisely how many clicked on which article for what length of time is in effect to give advertisers an idea of the exact value of their investment- all pretense at neutrality is out the window.

Serving NYT's loyal readers, the reporters didn't just report on possible causes and alternative explanations for the Texas power debacle (too early to determine conclusively at the time the piece appeared), but immediately concluded with authority reserved for the perspective favored by the paid subscribers of the paper

</td></tr>
</table>

"Part of the responsibility for the near-collapse of the state's electrical grid can be traced to the decision in 1999 to embark on the nation's most extensive experiment in electrical deregulation."[26]

This is artful framing. The fact that Oregon – regulated to the hilt - suffered from the collapse of its grid that same week was not mentioned. An error of omission is not as serious an offense as an error of commission (to fact-checkers delight). In another story by MSN about Oregon, the reporters made sure the distinction was clear: "The power outages experienced in the Willamette Valley over the past week are nothing like those experienced in Texas." Sitting in the dark and shivering in Oregon seems very much similar. The fact that California has suffered rolling blackouts every year or so since re-regulating in 2002 was overlooked artfully by stating the opposite: California had to re-regulate in 2002 because of market manipulation. Words are a weapon. Choosing the right ones makes a difference.

The reason NY Times' presentation was art was that most reasonable readers might have concluded – without the paper's perspective- that the opposite was more valid. Texas, notable for devastating heat waves, demonstrated the strength of market-based electric deregulation. During summer times, the system holds while California's re-re-re-regulated utility seems to cause some fires itself. The Texas utility companies didn't plan for a once-in-a-lifetime freeze. Neither did they prepare for a volcanic eruption or a Chinese takeover of Washington. The NYT biased perspective accused the Texas authorities of not equipping its wind turbines with expensive de-icing like North Dakota's; After all, North Dakota is also in the Milky Way Galaxy, aren't they? A different perspective would be that the market will adjust not because of regulations but because customers demand it. Independent-minded Texans will get generators, solar panels, batteries to decouple from the grid, just as Texas itself always played it alone. And electricity will be cheaper than regulated rates. But the NY Time's readers got what they wanted to hear.

Back to competitive intelligence: managers should present a perspective but shouldn't *be obviously biased.* Executives will immediately tune off if they see no silver ray. A delivery must pretend to be balanced *even if it is not.*

Since competitive intelligence is never about the facts- those are reserved for lower-level, tactical "good to know but useless" news items, the NY Times teaches how to do it well. It buried the other perspective in *one line*: "The state's entire energy infrastructure was walloped with glacial temperatures that even under the strongest of regulations might have frozen gas wells and downed power lines." This line might have proved its entire hypothesis about the failure of the market as false, so the NY Times moved on quickly.

Everything in the NY Times article was based on facts. It didn't lie to its readers. However, the facts didn't strongly support the conclusion. The conclusion was just one possible explanation. Other explanations were as likely (if not more so). Such manipulation is known as abductive reasoning.

Abductive reasoning (or abduction) moves from a set of observations or experiences into conclusions that are not totally backed by the evidence and instead are "best guess." Being one explanation out of several, they are often a conclusion favored by the concluder. Abductive reasoning differs from inductive reasoning, which uses sampling and testing to arrive at a highly probable inference.

There is no "truth" in competitive intelligence. It's not a cynical view; it's an admission that everything is seen through some interpreter's eyes. Choosing *what* to collect and distribute is subjective. When managers present to executives what they consider as opportunities for an edge, they must reckon with their perspective being just one likely interpretation of competitive development and that top management is looking for more realistic growth. Structuring a presentation according to abductive reasoning will not be dismissed as direct manipulation, and framing the conclusion as "best guess, "most likely "outcome," etc., will have *a chance to affect thinking.*

Chapter 15:
External Focus and Competitive Intelligence

Some data vendors pitch their wares to corporate buyers claiming greater efficiency in information collection needed by the decision-makers. Some even claim their software automates strategy making. This is false. Technology can automate data searches, but it can't automate the discovery of opportunities by market-facing managers. Strategy, in turn, rests on perspective – assumptions about the Big Picture. There is no automating of strategy or perspective.

Corporate is used to fads. In its increasingly desperate search for cost savings and growth findings, executives are prone to fall for fads rather than good old fashion common sense. Examples include DevOps and Design Thinking, to name a few.

Introduced around 2008, DevOps was a software development culture hailed as the savior in managing complex IT projects. Amazon AWS defined it as "the combination of cultural philosophies, practices, and tools that increases an organization's ability to deliver applications and services at high velocity: evolving and improving products at a faster pace than organizations using traditional software development and infrastructure management processes." Forrester issued a report extolling the benefits of Agile Dev Ops. Then a decade later, we hear Dev Ops isn't working, and Agile Dev Ops wasn't delivering business outcomes. The idea of faster development is common sense but what one develops is more important than how fast. As Peter Drucker comments somewhat drily, "Efficiency is doing things right; Effectiveness is doing the right things."

Then came Design Thinking. IBM hailed Design Thinking as the panacea to operational problems in complex systems.

Referring to a Forrester report, the benefits included increasing organizational ability to deliver products and services faster, cutting costs, improving outcomes, and saving the planet.

Sounds familiar?

Forrester's report from February 2018 is no longer available on the IBM site since apparently, my blog post caused it to disappear, or maybe an intern deleted it by mistake. However, ignoring the questionable assumptions behind its calculations reveals that only about 28% of the respondents to a survey said Design Thinking had become a sustainable change in their companies. So that is one more fad down the drain. "Efficiency is doing things right; Effectiveness is doing the right things."

Every few years, a new fad promising cultural change, cost saving, reduced time to market, fewer mistakes, and streamlined processes sweeps the business world, then dies quietly. Some make money off it, some spend money on it, and little changes.

It is time to do the right things: A cultural revolution regarding external focus and incentivizing mid-management and professionals to identify new profit opportunities. Unfortunately, when it comes to intelligence-seeking behavior, many companies still live in DOS 1.0 generation.

I am not against increasing efficiency in management. However, I am against the idea that efficiency is the panacea to competing. As long as strategy focuses on eliminating waste in design but not on eliminating waste in noise, not much will change despite all the efficiencies introduced into strategy making. The strategy process is messy because the world is messy, and insight is challenging. Software and efficiencies in strategy making do not make for better strategy, just for better claims about strategy.

A fundamental change requires opening channels for opportunity intelligence to flow.

All the ingredients are present in making *managers* locate opportunities without regards to efficiency:

- Does this practice make common sense? Check. What they see from here, executives and their high-level advisors do not see from there.
- Is it guaranteed to increase the number of growth opportunities? Check. In a world that is being upended from global to local, from Western-dominated to Asia-dominated, from open to closed, from free market to crony capitalism and massive government intervention, market-facing managers have an unparalleled front seat's view.
- Is it more effective and quicker than waiting for data and rear-view insight? Check. By the time McKinsey, BCG, Gartner, or Forrester write their "white papers, " the opportunity has moved on.

What's missing?

A different perspective of leadership teams and their executives that realizes technology is a *tool*, and people are the actual *asset*, and finding opportunities for technology to make a difference depends on management listening to its people.

The view from an EVP

The idea that companies should harvest market insights from a wide net of employees is slowly making its way to the top of corporations. Stan Sthanunathan, who served decades as Unilever's czar of consumer insights, suggests just that in an interview in 2021 with Gregg Archibald of Gen2 Advisors[27]: "Today, insights are the responsibility of the insights department. But tomorrow Insights should be everyone's responsibility."

Quick takeaways for the road:

> *Everyone quotes Peter Drucker, "Efficiency is doing things right; Effectiveness is doing the right things." Few do it. Quotes are easy!*

> *It's hard to believe but in some companies telling management to listen to its people is considered a breakthrough idea.*

> *"Today, insights are the responsibility of the insights department. But tomorrow insights should be everyone's responsibility." Stan Sthanunathan, formerly the Executive Vice President of Consumer and Market Insights at Unilever*

PART V:
A New Model for Competitive Intelligence

Chapter 16:
Cutting Down on Noise

A new perspective of leadership teams on competitive intelligence starts with cutting down on noise inside the company. The first step on cutting down the noise is... cutting down noise.

This is easier said than done due to FOMO/FOMU[28] and defensive decision-making. Luckily, recent research interest in the damaging effects of noise[29] by leading authorities on decision making might get management more serious about improving the situation. Noise clutters corporate formal information channels and significantly affects the rate of bad judgments. The authors of *Noise* popularized cognitive biases, but the reality is we are none better for knowing we have biases. So cutting down on noise might be a bit easier.

FOMO/FOMU is way more robust than the awareness of a problem, though. AI/ML platforms add an enormous quantity of data to the corporate knowledge system. In a way, the old Phoenician traders, waiting months to hear anything from their ships, might have been better off. They didn't have internet search but what they received from their merchants was only essential news, not Facebook/Twitter chats.

Unlike books devoted to describing the problem and then offering trivial advice to solve it (be kind, recycle, smile often), this book devotes most space to solving it. It describes a framework for System 1 to scan through the noise and pluck an item and then a framework for System 2 to follow up to foretell an opportunity.

This step was named the competitive intelligence quest. The next step is to elevate that quest to those who can make a decision about pursuing an opportunity.

People might be your best assets, but they produce a lot of noise

Most leaders are sincere in their belief that the true asset of their companies is their people, the teams, the collective effort. Harnessing that power of the collective, however, is far from simple. An executive in a large company can't pay attention to every manager's perspective on opportunities.

The conventional mechanism in large organizations to reduce noise is relying on hierarchy. Information is filtered through layers of management so that at the top, the amount is greatly reduced. Top executives augment their knowledge via their own trusted circle, mainly peer-level outsiders or fee-earning mercenaries of advice.

This process has been working well for decades until it stopped working. With the advent of data availability, it is breaking down. It is simply inhuman to follow all leads. Decision-support platforms never worked well, to begin with, and nowadays, strategy "dashboards" aren't much better when looking ahead and identifying opportunities. They do serve some purpose of looking back and using outcomes to make judgments, but as the authors of Noise suggest, these are no longer effective ways to improve decisions.

Technology will help. The specific technology, however, is explicitly geared towards cutting down on noise. That leaves out most data-based platforms such as news aggregators or market "intelligence." Algorithms that "hide" Big Data by offering patterns and predictions are useful in cutting down on noise, but few of them exist outside consumption-based models of customers' behavior. Executives, moreover, still derive their perspectives of customers' changing needs by *talking* to big accounts.

The worst offenders are Customer Relationship Management platforms (CRM). An invention that propelled Salesforce.com to a multibillion powerhouse is as ubiquitous today as appointment books were a century ago, but they run into humans.

The most impatient humans: salespeople.

Having all the customer's info at the screen in front of a service agent is helpful for contact centers that are the core of service providing. Salespeople should be natural consumers of CRM information but rarely to the full extent. After a while, it becomes just more noise.

That fact didn't escape the entrepreneurial perspective of two Israelis- Amit Ben-Dov and Eilon Reshef, who founded Gong.

The idea behind Gong is that CRM doesn't work as well as one hopes. In the words of Ben-Dov:

 "CRM systems make very poor systems of engagement. While they contain a wealth of information for business leadership, getting staff to *put information into them or utilize the information that's in them* is an ongoing battle[30]." (Italics added)

In 1988, when I co-authored the first-ever book to propose organizing a systematic intelligence process[31], our advice to companies was to create an internal network of collectors, and first and foremost, try and get salespeople to contribute. The book sold out, which started my career (and the formal creation of competitive intelligence jobs) and was adopted wholeheartedly by Fortune 500.

The advice about salespeople, though, was crap.

Oh, sorry, offensive language. The advice was terrible. It was highly unimplementable in the face of salespeople's fluidity of attention to simultaneous signals in their immediate environment about emerging competitive issues.

Salespeople just didn't contribute anything despite all incentive schemes and top management urging. You could twist their arms, hold a gun to their head (not literally), but they still had no time for competitive intelligence reporting and hardly paid attention to the competitive professional asking for it (let alone the HQ marketers). The simple explanation was that the incentive of selling more outweighs all the puny incentives (or penalties) designed by management.

Now one software called Gong can change that in a hurry.

Real intelligence

The main selling point and competitive advantage of Gong are that unlike other data platforms, it reduces noise.

Gong created a new space called Revenue Intelligence. The difference between intelligence and data, more data, and even more data is what one does with all that data. Comments from participants in our training suggest one does very little. Data are not insights.

Unlike CRM, which collects tons of data about existing customers, improves "relationships" with them, and reduces the cost of sales, or "market intelligence" platforms that contain tons of data about competitors or markets, Gong's focus is insights to increase revenues. Gong does it by automating the capture of and finding patterns in all conversations between salespeople and existing or prospective customers in the B2B space. In the process, it can also flag competitive weaknesses, and gaps glanced from the prospect-salesperson conversation. Finally, it funnels all data into opportunities for upselling, prediction of deal closure, and options to increase the probability of a sale.

In other words, it's not more data; it's fewer data. So if we define intelligence as *generating options for an edge,* Gong implements that definition.

Ben-Dov and his cofounder- Eilon Reshef - didn't look at every detail and feature of Salesforce or Dynamics 360, the two leading CRM systems. Instead, they saw pain points for salespeople and realized these weren't about *too little information.* What was missing was a filter that generated specific options for these salespeople about opportunities.

Competitive strategy is about distinguishing your offering from the competition. For that, one doesn't need 175 Zettabyte of information about every burp by a competitor, just enough knowledge to be different. In the search for opportunities, technology such as Gong's offers a promising start. It reduces noise, on the one hand, and generates insights on the other. While these insights are geared towards salespeople, they are not limited to salespeople. Since one source for identifying gaps in the market are customers and prospective customers, the technology generates information that *might* add to a manager's quest for early signals of change and resulting opportunities.

It is hard for corporations to move away from the notion that competitive intelligence is just a "baby monitor" for competitors. Replacing this outmoded idea with a focus on the evolution of industries and their high-power players (not just competitors) requires management to admit that it is not in total control over the outcomes of its moves. Call it humility, call it confronting reality, or call it business acumen: It is an asset.

Many companies misunderstand that and waste their search for opportunities on tactical details that don't move the needle. Strategy is not about chasing competitors but attempting to stay one step ahead of them with a new edge. Not surprising, Marc Benioff, the godfather of CRM, is among the early investors in Gong who explicitly criticizes CRMs, Salesforce.com's core revenue generator. Benioff knows intelligence when he sees it.

One of Gong's early clients was Slack, the cloud-based internal collaboration tool. Who now owns Slack? You guessed it: Saleforce.com.

Technology's limits

Gong's technology is great but has one potential limitation: it will improve the current strategy but might not change top management's perspective. It is part of executing more effectively- a practice Michael Porter named *Operational Effectiveness*. It is an absolute requirement for bottom-line improvement, but it is not a long-term guarantee of growth. Discovering new signals of change in the market that others ignore requires a different approach. If customers know about it, it might already be late.

Gong shows the way on a tactical, sales-oriented level. What companies need, desperately it seems, in a world where growth opportunities seem to dwindle, is a similar approach but at a strategic level. Of course, creating an edge via a competitive intelligence hunt requires more than improving current strategy, but Gong shows the way: *Cut down on noise.* Any software that follows will have to reckon with Gong's genius.

Quick takeaways for the road:

An executive in a large company can't pay attention to every manager's perspective on opportunities. A company needs a more systematic approach to tapping its market-facing front line managers' alertness.

Replacing this outmoded idea of competitive intelligence as a "baby monitor" for competitors, requires management to admit to itself that it is not in total control over outcomes of its moves. Humility is an asset.

Chapter 17:
A New Approach to Competitive Intelligence

The flow of competitive intelligence inside an organization is never smooth. Since the Fortune 500 adopted a systematic competitive intelligence process following the *Business Intelligence System* book, the model has revealed several weaknesses and yet surprising resilience.

Sometimes, resilience is not a good sign.

The original model called for a centralized intelligence function with analysts and collectors, supported by an internal network of sources who come across competitive bits during their routine work. As discussed earlier, the model failed to get active and sustained participation in the network. The reasons ranged from

- lack of incentives,
- lack of measurable effect on decisions,
- one-way flow with negligible benefits for the individual contributor taking part in it, and
- top executives' disinterest in tapping subordinates for perspectives.

The Internal Network idea died, with only a few companies with unique collaborative culture (Ericsson, Royal Dutch Shell) keeping some resemblance of it for several decades longer. The rest of the corporate world moved to total reliance on secondary sources (published or private) or vendors/consultants/ investment bankers for opportunity intelligence.

The next phase in the quest to increase the availability of competitive intelligence to decision-makers pushed the function into the business units, closer to the market, and focused on competitor tactical data, serving mostly marketing, business development, and sales teams. The advent of storage and distribution platforms made this revised model resilient, and it is still the dominant model in Western companies despite some glaring deficiencies.

Looking back at the state of competitive intelligence in the 80s and today, it is clear the function has made great strides in improving its tools and products. The add-on from analytical products (Big Data and predictive analytics included) and the sophistication of search and distribution platforms, compared to the nominal technology that was available in the 80s, make today's information products magnitude better than the old paper reports. However, despite several benefits of this model, and its widespread adoption across the Fortune companies, its limitations are obvious:

1. The focus on competitors is the wrong focus. Competitors are just one influencing players in the evolution of sectors. 'Competitive' is not synonymous with competitors. Still, most companies feel comfortable with clear designation along functional lines: Competitive intelligence deals with competitors, market research deals with customers, M&A deals with potential acquisitions, Business Development deals with new sales opportunities for existing products and services and so on. Companies write the demarcation lines in stone. Silos are protected fiercely. Top executives complain routinely about silos, yet their own insistence on clear boundaries creates them.

2. The focus on tactical data adds to the noise. "Good to know" flows do little to reveal opportunities for an edge but clog recipients' emails.

3. Users are primarily middle management – product, brand, and project - and they provide little helpful feedback of the actual effect of competitive input on their own market perspectives. They also overall fail to communicate change in their perspectives back to the formal "CI function."

4. Top executives' use is severely limited, sporadic, and at times random (i.e., the professionals have no idea what management will see as relevant).

In sum, while the sophistication and productivity of information production have risen significantly, *the impact on opportunity discovery has not*. We can trace it to the de-sensitization of the recipients with the constant deluge of news, updates, developments, warnings, and alerts. In other words, the failure of a formal competitive intelligence function is ironically tied to their success in producing and delivering too much information.

The sclerotic channels

The aptest analogy to describe the state of noise inside a large organization compares the communication channels to deteriorating arteries in a human body, where blood flow is restricted by plaques on blood vessels' walls (known as arteriosclerosis).

There are several possible courses of treatment in the case of arteriosclerosis, and they have analogous "treatments" in organizations

1. Scrapping the sides of the artery to remove the plaque or changing diets to prevent further buildup. Corporate analogy calls for management to mandate the lowering of

noise by edicts such as maximum time limit on meetings, restricted distribution lists on emails, etc. Alternatively, management can use a "noise audit" such as suggested by the authors of *Noise* and cut down on subscriptions, databases, the proliferation of useless platforms, etc.

In human arteriosclerosis, removing plaque is dangerous as it can lead to embolism (a chunk of removed plaque clogging a critical blood vessel leading to stroke or heart attack). Inside corporations FOMO (Fear of Missing Out by management) and FEMU (Fear of Messing Up by subordinates) will all but guarantee the failure of the policy over the long run. Meetings will slowly drift back to hours of discussions; reports will grow in volumes, distribution lists will re-populate. It's just human nature. Alternative to scraping vessels is--

2. Expanding the artery. This is a well-known treatment using drugs, balloon-stents, and even exercise regimes. In companies, expanding the capacity of channels is carried out via technology such as sharing platforms (SharePoint, Google Drive) and communications apps (e.g., Slack). The problem with these treatments is that just like traffic, *noise expands to fill the expanded channels.*

3. In cases of severe arteriosclerosis, surgeons will perform *a bypass*.

The bypass model: A radical change in the management use of competitive intelligence

The "bypass" model represents a new approach to competitive intelligence for companies interested in growth. The model has significant promise. It has been in use among several leading companies (in Energy, Defense, and Pharmaceuticals). It has a proven track record and several advantages, though its implementation can run into political issues that require management commitment to fight silos and inspire managers. It requires a determined top executive at whose behest the model operates.

Figure 8 details the empirical basis for opening a "bypass" channel. Since finding opportunities is meaningless if these never make it to the top for approval, and the top never gets to send feedback about what and why (or why not) they were interested, a bypass channel that completes the feedback loop is the most critical element in overcoming noise.

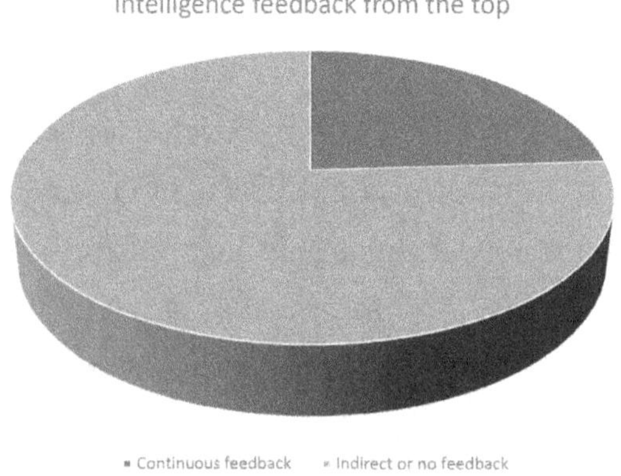

Figure 8: "How much do you know about top management use of your reports?" N=291

Figure 8 above is based on responses from 291 intelligence professionals in large companies in a 2019 survey[32]. Intelligence producers receive very little feedback to calibrate their search for opportunities in the market. The sample of close to 300 respondents included both professionals whose main task was to "hunt" and middle managers who ran across what they considered useful competitive information but never or only occasionally received feedback on the usefulness of their discovery.

That state of flow is clearly not optimal for the healthy growth of an enterprise.

In the business enterprise, chocked with noise, a bypass model is called the "Briefer-based bypass model" or, in short, the Briefer Model. This book, for the first time, presents a complete illustration of this model. Eventually, based on the widespread adoption of the 1988 original model, I anticipate that most large companies will drift towards a BBBM in some form (though with different speeds depending on their industries).

The Briefer-Based Bypass Model (BBBM) for competitive intelligence

"The Briefer" model is an adaptation from national security intelligence, with a big caveat. The fact that the BBB model derives from the intelligence community's experience doesn't mean competitive and national intelligence have much in common. They don't, but for the term "intelligence." The term "intelligence" is, however, itself grossly misleading.

In military/government use, intelligence stands for an enemy's secrets obtained without its consent. There is no commonality whatsoever with market intelligence which is neither about secrets nor obtained illegally. The term intelligence in this book is clearly *useful information about the competitive edge* a manager or an analyst glimpse in their daily tasks. No James Bond or George Smiley, or even Edward Snowden here.

It is illegal to obtain "intelligence" (as in secrets) in business which means that industrial espionage is *not* competitive intelligence. Beyond the legal aspect, though, competitive intelligence is market insight, and as Chapter 16 suggests, one of the best sources is a company's salespeople talking to customers and prospects. What "secrets" can provide a company with an edge? If you discovered Coca-Cola's formula (a trade secret for a century), would you be able to compete with it?

A skeptical reader may note that China, which has been systematically ripping off IP on an industrial scale, seems to be able to use industrial espionage to beat Western firms. That is true, but the edge has been in the Chinese ability to produce the same products cheaper and faster, protect their market (illegally) with government-created barriers, and force technology transfer on short-sighted Western companies. China has been significantly helped by complacent Western governments, short-sighted or incompetent CEOs, and even more short-sighted Wall Street investors and uninformed stock analysts. The IP itself was never enough to give China an edge. Huawei came to dominate 5G after stealing the IP from Nortel and Alcatel-Lucent, the failing Canadian companies, but then improving on it so much that Western firms just couldn't catch up[32]. Industrial espionage allows a country to imitate quickly, but the competitive edge is outside espionage's reach.

So why borrow a model from national intelligence? One common issue facing information flows in government and commercial corporations alike is that Noise is clogging the system. So how to reach and affect decision makers' perspectives may be the only thing worthy of learning from the government.

The following statement should qualify even the recommended model in the next pages: Neither Obama nor Trump used intelligence. Neither changed perspective because of intelligence. George Bush (the son) used false "intelligence" on nonexistent Weapons of Mass Destruction (WMD) to justify the war in Iraq. Relying on a government model is not an endorsement of a particular administration's appreciation for inconvenient perspectives. It's still better, however than the current state of sclerosis in corporate communication channels.

The current prevailing channel-bypass used by the US national security community to (try and) affect a President's perspectives is a PDB- Presidential Daily Brief mechanism. Briefing a President is a revered *institution*, well-funded, and enjoying tremendous prestige. It's done regularly, every morning, by a Briefer who is backed by a dedicated team in the intelligence community but *independent of its bureaucracy and formal channels.*

The briefer must form a special bond of trust with the President. While they are in constant contact with all high-level functionaries (cabinet ministers, military leaders), their sole loyalty is to the President.

It is hard to be a Briefer to someone who doesn't want to listen. So the first condition to importing the "bypass" model to corporations is to make sure the audience (either a corporate

CEO or a Business Unit's President) is receptive to the idea. A "wishy-washy" consent is not enough.

The second condition is to select a person who is trusted by that top executive and respected by lower echelons. During Donald Trump's presidency, the Briefer *de facto* was Mike Pompeo, his Secretary of Defense, Trump's only consistently trusted advisor. No one else had Trump's ear. The betrayal of Trump by the various heads of intelligence under Obama left him rightly suspicious of the loyalty of that community.

The rationale for a corporate Briefer

Even the most down-to-earth corporate leader can't interact with every manager in their organization. So filtering information is a must. The problem arises when filtering via the formal channels leaves top management deprived of early signals of opportunities.

Some leaders will vehemently deny being the "last to know." For a while, top executives attempted to gain some control over what information reached them using "managing by walking around." That MBWA trend died a quiet death as it was incredibly time consuming, riddled with random interactions, and unhelpful to the executive beyond the health benefit of walking.

In the next chapter, I show a chart presenting the different stages in the maturity of competitive intelligence processes. The MBWA fits into the lower right quadrant; it did raise feedback, but it was of little real value to the user.

I am not a fan of Gartner's Magic Quadrant, especially since quadrant means just one block in the chart, but Gartner uses the term for the whole chart, which may suggest a problem in their geometry or a magic a la Harry Potter. But there is some magic in the "sense-making" quadrant: it is the most effective mature model of affecting perspectives at the top when it works.

Quick takeaways for the road:

> *A bypass channel that completes the feedback loop is the most critical element in overcoming noise and developing opportunity intelligence.*

> *Relying on government models in any area of life is risky at best. It's still better than the current state of sclerosis in corporate communication channels.*

Chapter 18:
The CI-Maturity Magic Quadrant

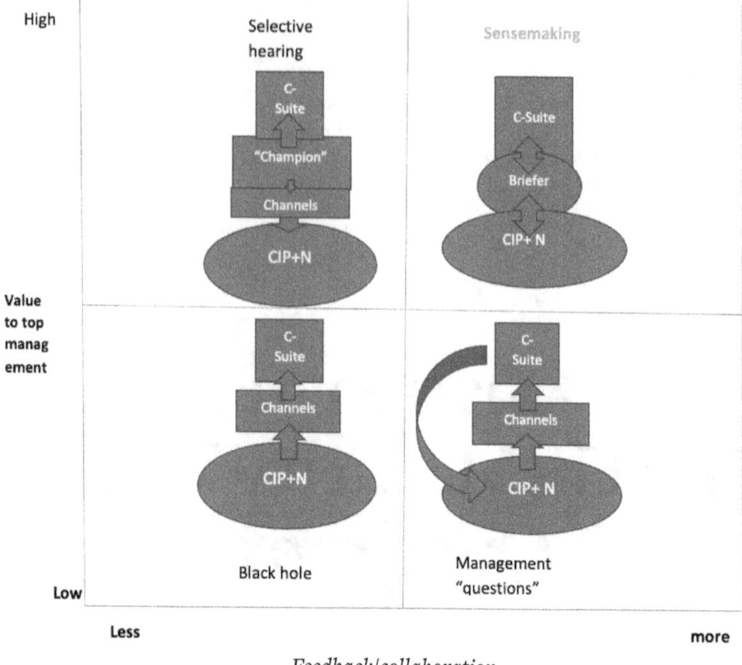

Figure 10: The "Magic Quadrant" of corporate strategic intelligence

The Black-Hole model

Most companies' common state of competitive intelligence is the "black hole" (lower left quadrant). A professional analyst (CIP™) or market-facing managers (N= Network) move competitive information through formal channels. The channels filter both irrelevant and relevant-but-inconvenient information such as early signs the strategy isn't working or opening of opportunities that are too "out there" for corporate comfort. What reaches the top typically conforms to operational details with little value in identifying strategic opportunities. Instead, executives receive information about possible opportunities from their own circle of trusted advisors. These include outside parties such as senior partners in large consulting firms, investment bankers, board members, and at times, peers in non-competing companies. Some of these parties have an obvious financial interest in presenting deals as opportunities when they aren't (investment bankers, consultants) or promoting their own agenda (board members). The entrepreneurial managers who float possible opportunities and see no feedback and no action are left to wonder about the benefit of their effort. Over time, the flow of market insights from a motivated workforce dwindles to nothing. One common symptom that your company has reached that level is the acceptance by middle managers of "complacence," risk-averse, slow-to-act culture as just the fact of life. Leaders' speeches about the importance of agility are secretly mocked as empty slogans. Moreover, given the impossibility of directly assessing what management finds as relevant signals, competitive intelligence flows are solely restricted to early warning about risks based on FEMU (Fear of Messing Up).

<table>
<tr><td>

Case in Point

A leading company in a scientific field has been experiencing a slow decline in its market share as competitors- one much larger and one with a lower cost structure have been squeezing it on both sides. The company had been very profitable for many years. Rising competition, therefore, should have been expected. However, slowing down the deteriorating performance was left to salespeople who were supposed to convince clients to follow the life cycle of their products with the new generation of the same products from this company. Instead, customers began replacing this company's expensive (though higher quality) products with cheaper alternatives. The company has been slowly but clearly "pushed" into a niche where its premium products were absolutely necessary for clients' performance. A modification of the legacy strategy rather than a tactical battle for customers was required, but management failed to adapt. An acquisition (the classic attempt to revive a flagging strategy) didn't produce the hope-for

</td></tr>
</table>

turnaround. Then a new CEO from a related field was installed. His track record included reviving the fortunes of a business owned by a cash-rich giant company. While it was clear why the board looked for the magic of "turnaround" record, the superficial analogy – he succeeded there, he would succeed here- is not uncommon in hiring CEOs[34].

You'd think a new CEO would be interested in the perspectives of his managers as to how to stem the decline of the company. Instead, this new CEO censored an internal report about the flagging strategy that presented a reality check. A lone competition analyst identified an opportunity to block the low-cost competitor while holding off the more significant competitor through "taking the battle" to their territory. The idea was to cause this much larger competitor to expend resources fighting his company, thereby rethinking the push against it as less profitable. His reports went into a black hole. While this was definitely within management's rights not to accept, the total lack of feedback caused middle managers to reduce upward communication of "bad news" to a minimum. As I write this book, the company's decline continues unabated. Rumors had it the CEO was looking to sell it- and the board may have selected him precisely for his record in selling a previous company. Morale is at a low point.

Instead of modifying his strategy, the CEO announced an ambitious sales target that included no new initiatives, no breakthrough products, and no recognition of new opportunities brought on by a "transformation" team. He might be able to sell the company and even receive a bonus for selling it, but his black-hole practice didn't bode well for his reputation as a turn-around expert. The idea behind turnaround is first to put the company on a growth path and then sell it at a premium. Unfortunately, black-hole models do not encourage a meaningful search for growth opportunities.

Management-Questions model

The so-called "management questions" refers to a one-way communication whereby competitive intelligence is sought only for specific issues without explanation or context and without regard to any additional insights the professional analyst or the market-facing manager might provide. Black-Hole and Management (mostly random) Questions are at times combined into a model where top executives bypass official channels and send requests for data directly to the professional or the manager but without providing any clues as to the reasoning behind the demand for more information.

Every competitive intelligence manager in a large company is familiar with this model. First, attempts to provide context (see chapter 6) are rebuffed with "feedback" such as "just the facts, please" or "you don't need to know more." Soon, managers learn to avoid providing anything more than raw data.

Case in Point

A food company's scientists developed a breakthrough, first-in-class product that received a lukewarm response from top executives. The company was well known as risk-averse, uncomfortable with anything outside its known areas, focused on production, and happy to stay that way. The company was large, dominant in its segment, facing only one other, even larger competitor, and comfortable with its mediocre performance where it expected growth in single digits. The company was part of a colossal parent company spanning a diverse portfolio.

In a strategy workshop, participants highlighted some reservations regarding the complexity of launching this particular product with which the company had little experience. This product offered a different approach to a widespread problem, yet the champion of the product and her team met with skepticism at every turn. Management wanted to know in advance what the response of some stakeholders will be, including a group that had only a marginal effect on the product and how and whom will be using it. Obviously, management was scared, and its questions focused on narrow issues, not the bigger picture.

The team fought for two years to gain acceptance for a launch that will make waves. Management demurred. It wanted a small, incremental approach to minimize risks, but that approach would have also killed the initiative's breakthrough potential. Management wanted much more data. Ironically, expertise in another part of the parent company could have solved many of the issues. Still, management didn't seek the perspective of experts from that business. It was typical of the silos in large companies. The launch was delayed by two years until management agreed to take a chance on the opportunity.

The opportunity was evident to everyone but top management. When the company launched the product, at last, it became a sensation on a global scale with a coordinated campaign. At least there was a happy ending.

Selective Hearing model

In the selective hearing model, a champion higher up in the hierarchy takes an interest in the flow of intelligence. The sponsor can be a VP or even an SVP closer to the leadership team than middle management or the professional intelligence function.

Particulars differ depending on the location of the champion and their extent of interest in receiving intelligence. The arrangement described below is for a typical large company

The champion, often part of the executive circle, is familiar with strategic discussions at the top. They then confer with the relevant bosses in charge of the area where an intelligence function may reside (or to which an enterprising manager with an idea of an emerging opportunity reports). For example, an

EVP Strategy may discuss issues with the CMO, who has three VPs under her. One of those VPs being in charge, among other areas, of the function of intelligence and analytics (this is based on a real company, but keep in mind the model is idiosyncratic-companies have at times bizarre reporting structures). The CMO then calls on the VP, who calls on the director of competitive intelligence and relays the EVP's issues/concerns/interests. Thus, the intelligence function now has a "champion" to channel its analysis of emerging opportunities.

The advantage of this model is that the flow upward has a *chance* of reaching the top via the said champion who is senior enough to bring it up with the inner leadership circle. And while the feedback loop is not exactly smooth and efficient – a trickle of downstream briefing at the champion leisure- it is better than no feedback.

The nature of the exchange between the champion and the boss informing the analysts or middle managers of senior executives' perspectives varies greatly. Politics, egos, and limited time for a genuine dialogue typically restrict the flow downward. Managers' understanding, vital for assessing what will constitute opportunities when proposed to the leadership team and the champion, is therefore partial.

Another flaw in this model is that champions come and go, and when they leave, so leaves the communication channel. Moreover, their interest is often limited chiefly to their area of responsibility. That leaves the analysts with a "tunnel vision" of what's going on upstairs.

Case in Point

In a very famous, dominant, European giant, competitive intelligence has never been of great interest to management. More accurately, interest spiked and waned over the years. As the competitive climate around the whole industry changed drastically over time, efforts to revive the appeal of CI to its early glory days received an unexpected boost. A very senior executive on the leadership team with a direct line to the CEO grew louder in insisting the company had very little useful information about the competition. Her protestation erupted in one top executive meeting when she insisted on getting better "intelligence" and demanded the company hire a large consulting firm to study the intelligence processes in the company and advice on how to reorganize them.

The consulting firm with expertise in reorganization but not in intelligence flows proposed an ambitious project with steps and layers and made far-reaching recommendations. Management accepted none of these recommendations, and the project died. The cost of the project was minuscule to the giant. The cost of failure to revive intelligence flows may be way higher.

The executive champion in this case was a CFO. Her interest was in financial benchmarking, not strategic opportunities. Benchmarking a champion whose focus is on imitating others is not much better than no champion at all.

Sensemaking model

Our studies showed that feedback was one of three most (statistically) significant factors in affecting management perspective. They imply that any model must tackle this issue head-on. The maturity of opportunity intelligence in a company doesn't depend on how sophisticated the product has become. Instead, it is rooted in how much the company uses the information, which revolves around an effective feedback loop.

This "revolutionary" perspective on the optimal model for market insight into growth opportunities is a radical departure from the existing model in Corporate America and years ahead of Corporate Europe. A mature and effective model is the open, structured, and honest dialogue between the top user and the intelligence providers via an officially designated role of a **briefer** who has one foot in the intel producers' community and one foot at the executive inner circle. The Daily Presidential Briefing in government circles provides that model.

What can we learn from the US Presidential Briefing?

Can you imagine being the liaison between President Trump and the intelligence community (all 17 agencies of it)? Given the bad blood, the job of this liaison – who oversaw the briefing of President Trump – was an art of walking on a tight rope, at 100 feet above the ground, with no safety net. Trump himself said he didn't need a daily brief. He might have been right. His grasp of what mattered (China, safe borders, staying out of wars) was that of a businessman, not a politician. The liberal mainstream media might have vilified him, but his perspective (if not demeanor and tweets) for the most part was better than his predecessor's.

Former President Obama immediately chided Trump for skipping the daily brief, saying it made him *fly blind*, but his record was as bad. Obama skipped more than half of his briefs in his first term and up until the ISIS crisis in his second term. His team claimed he preferred reading over an oral brief. However, the value of the daily brief has always been in the *verbal exchange* where the President gets to ask questions, probe assumptions, and deeply understand others' perspectives. Body language, tone, and facial expressions play an important role in conveying the urgency and importance of issues.

As stated earlier in this book, the task of briefing VIPs – in government *or* in business- requires a delicate balancing act of *staying true to the analysis* and *accommodating the decision maker's agenda and perspectives.* Adrian Wolfberg, an organizational change consultant and a former senior intelligence officer with the DIA, describes in a recent article the main task of the presidential daily brief as *sensemaking*[35]. Sensemaking in the intelligence realm is not about facts and not about truths, and not about accuracy. It is an interpretation of events. Since the days of President George H. Bush, it has been carried out face-to-face as a dialogue between the briefer and the decision-maker. However, when we think of "sensemaking" in a typical corporate system, its direction is always from the top down with little or no dialogue (Black-Hole or Management Questions models).

The role of sensemaking requires unique freedoms not typically afforded by hierarchical systems like a Fortune 500 firm. Given the enormous power asymmetry between the briefed (a very senior decision-maker) and the briefer (a competitive intelligence professional or a market-facing manager), current briefing practices (presentation at executive retreats?) afford little value. Suppose the briefer is to work within the corporate rules. In that case, their immediate boss and all the layers up to the top will "sanitize" their messages to fit *their* understanding of what should reach top management. This is known as "window dressing" and is a widespread and unavoidable process in most companies. Incentives for window dressing are way more powerful than incentives for an open flow of information.

The solution adopted by the US intelligence community was to create a *parallel* system that doesn't play by the same rules as the official system but supplements it. I call it a "bypass" solution mimicking the treatment of arteriosclerosis in the cardiovascular system.

Briefers carry out the sensemaking with unparalleled freedom of movement between the intelligence analysts and the policy makers' staff. The value of the briefer depends critically on the VIP having complete trust in them and the freedom the briefer enjoys from formal communication hierarchies.

It's not uncommon to find official and unofficial communication flows co-existing side by side in large firms. For example, executives at times tap a trusted senior salesperson or account executive to get a direct feel of "what actually is going out there." This parallel system, however, is at best haphazard, and therefore unsystematic. Such an unofficial communication channel is OK for tactical or operational purposes where clarity (of a situation) is easier to attain. Strategic intelligence, however, is not about tactical facts. Strategic intelligence is about interpreting the perspectives of customers, competitors, and regulators on the outside (to mention a few); On the inside, unfiltered views of country managers, researchers, and even executive team members add up. Diversity of perspectives is essential in market insight about opportunities, the focus of this book. Without a CEO or a unit President sanctioning the role of a briefer, there is no reason to believe such a channel can survive internal politics.

Uncertainty reduction has a price

A brief at times poses more questions than answers. Unlike tactical information, market insight is not ever clear-cut. Will Amazon "kill" the retail food business? Is Google going to be broken up by anti-trust? Will drug prices eventually come under government control? Is the new competitor's solution a true disruption? Competitive intelligence/market insight is never about accuracy; Different perspectives place market developments in context, and context allow better judgment calls, but it's not a crystal ball.

Most executives, however, want maximum uncertainty reduction. The price of that is eliminating options, both on the opportunity side and regarding potential disruption threats. Yet decision-makers need a *richer* set of scenarios and interpretations to prepare their organizations for more than one possible future. Shunning uncertainty via demands for more data and more accuracy is equivalent to demanding that a Las Vegas casino tilts the odds in your favor. Unfortunately, the world doesn't operate this way.

The Briefer Model in the administration is one example of how top decision-makers use intelligence. Unfortunately, intelligence usage at the highest levels is a relatively neglected area because researchers have limited access to top-level users. Adrian Wolfberg was the rare exception, and in another article, he interviewed top military commanders regarding their use of intelligence. He identified three dilemmas for intelligence producers that have parallels within the corporate environment. I am paraphrasing his observations in corporate terms.

- First, sense giving or sensemaking flows from the subordinate-to-superior direction, opposite the superior-to-subordinate direction found in hierarchical systems.
- Second, sensemaking must bridge the gap between strategy and intelligence, but the typical dominance of the operational topics makes the latter divorced from the former.
- Third, sensemaking across organizational silos thrives in non-hierarchical conditions.

The words of two of the generals interviewed by Wolfberg strike a special note to the theme of growth opportunity discovery and competing under noisy conditions:

"I needed a conceptual understanding. The problem was that people are focused on the day-to-day events... We break things down to understand the pieces but do a bad job of integrating them back up... We need to be able to rearrange things differently, to get different perspectives, and we need to provide incentives to do this, to reward people for this."

That same general added:

"Intelligence is really important because it is related to decisions that the commander has to make. What is the enemy doing? What are our own forces doing? What are my options? That is what intelligence is for; it is to understand how options can be pursued. We don't think like that, unfortunately. We are not connecting strategic intelligence with decisions and operations."

Finally, here is a leader who understands that in any organization, discovering opportunities depends on a wide network of eyes and ears, not just a few external consultants.

"I had a friend who told me there are three types of people: those who create options; those who sustain options; and those who give away options. Those who give away options should be fired. But options can come from anywhere: from combat arms, from combat support, and from combat service support. Intelligence is your whole operation. The critical piece is the understanding of the whole picture, and that is what you need intelligence for".[36]

I couldn't have said it better. "Those who give away options should be fired."

I concur, but it is easier said than done in Corporate.

Sensemaking in the commercial enterprise

Adapting the Briefer model to business is not straightforward since the relationship between a CEO and his top executives is not as hierarchical as in an administration/military. For example, Trump might have been able to dismiss advisors at the drop of a hat, but in business, top executives enjoy more power, support of board members and the investment community, and a CEO can't (and shouldn't) just push them aside. "Those who give away options should be fired" is absolutely correct but not always feasible.

To adapt the bypass model to the enterprise, one needs four pillars:

- The Briefer, by his position within the hierarchy, has the ear of the CEO/President and their complete trust. It can be a high-level expert respected for her record or a staffer working closely with the leader for a long time and on whom the leader relies. Being designated a Briefer is not a full-time position, and it *doesn't require additional resources.*

- The Briefer enjoys the trust of the market-facing managers and professional competition analysts by virtue of having no formal authority over them and no apparent political agenda of their own. They must speak the language of strategies (though not necessarily be in a strategy role) and be inclined by personality to see the big picture. Tactical, details-oriented briefers do not do well in this position since opportunities at the outset are vague by default and surrounded by uncertainty. That also rules out staffers who spent their professional lives solely in administrative roles removed from the actual business, even if they have the leader's trust. A briefer must be able to appreciate the potential market insight and, at the same time, be skeptical and analytical enough to weed out the noise.

- The interaction between the Briefer and the intelligence producers (professionals and market-facing managers) must be regular but not very frequent. Most strategic opportunities do not disappear if their relay takes two weeks. Too many meetings will make it impractical for a busy briefer who, unlike government employees, holds a "day job."

- The nature of the discourse between a Briefer and the intelligence producing managers must be well planned. It has a clear goal: a dialogue, not a lecture, and an open and honest exchange based on trust, not rank. It should include the following elements:
  - Summary of significant developments/emerging insights by the managers and professionals, within a time limit that cuts down on too many details
  - Questions from the Briefer and directions for further development of a "roadmap" to bringing the insight into focus on growth, with bottom-line impact
  - Briefing of top management's perspectives and shifting interests aimed at marking broad "boundaries" for market insights that have a probability of maturing into options
  - Questions from the managers of top management's initiatives
  - Clear timetable for next stage "signposts" for early signals

While conferring with intelligence producers regularly, the meetings serve the dual purpose of briefing the community of top management's shifting perspectives and keeping it always in the loop. Meeting with the Briefer merges individual managers' market insights and delivers clear feedback on what works and what doesn't and *why*. Without this feedback, this model is no better than the others.

In a large energy company with close to 45,000 employees worldwide and several business areas, the Briefer is the Chief Economist. Respected for her expertise, with a keen understanding of the nature of energy business, highly educated and relied on by the top executive, the Briefer enjoys the trust of both the top, the professional intelligence producers, and an extensive internal network designated as "market experts." The experts know that if she likes an idea, they will get recognition from the top echelon. The professional producers – a small team of 6 – benefit from the Briefer's regular feedback and mentoring. At the same time, the CEO knows the Briefer is well connected inside and outside the company, which benefits him. The Briefer has recently moved from informal communication to a structured schedule of meetings with a selected group from each business area, serving as a gateway into their broader market-facing communities.

If we discount the hype of direct and immediate causal effect on performance, it is still impossible not to be impressed with the performance of this company. While the energy business is volatile, this energy company is one of the most solid performers in the market. Against a backdrop of "alternative energy" hype by rivals, it stays committed to profitable sales rather than money-losing ventures. It is divesting lower profitability assets, reducing debt below its rivals' level, and plans – as its CEO says- to be profitable even under a low-price scenario for oil and gas. Before Corona shut down most of the world's fuel consumption, the company was the most profitable in its sector and even weathered the depression of 2020 well. It is now back to profitability. Is it due to the intelligence bypass route? I can't prove it. Is the bypass a better model than a black hole? You bet.

A manufacturer of construction material employs a different model. The director of Business Development serves as the Briefer, meeting with the CEO at the latter's home on the weekend for an informal brief and a debrief. The company doesn't have a professional competitive intelligence function, but the director is well connected inside and outside and serves as the nexus for the intelligence flow.

Both examples rely on the same principle. The Briefer is not an official position but a designated role enjoying the trust of both the top executive and the network of field managers and experts. A simple, inexpensive solution to a stubborn problem choking companies' growth.

How do managers find out about the Briefer?

The Briefer can be a formal designation (as in part of the description of that person's responsibility) or not, but the leader must fully accept it. Whether or not to inform the whole organization depends on the preference of the Briefer and the senior exec they brief. This preference depends primarily on two considerations: noise level and politics.

In the constantly fluid politics of large corporations, executives come and go, move from one position to another, and join and leave internal coalitions depending on issues. The Briefer may be a threat to the power of some of these functionaries. They may resent the trust of the CEO/Business unit head, disagree with the briefing, or want to *know in advance* what options the Briefer brings to the top.

In government circles, the Briefer confers with top appointments regularly and always includes their perspectives in briefing the President. In business, the "no surprise" culture is as strong, and the power of the top executives under a CEO might be stronger than the power of cabinet appointees around a President. It is, therefore, absolutely in a CEO's interest to make sure a Briefer doesn't antagonize others at the top. It is a delicate job, not for the faint of hearts. Therefore, a formal designation is an issue of how the CEO regards the political infighting around them.

The pro of a formal designation is that it elevates the importance of opportunity intelligence to its rightful place in an organization's quest for profitable growth. The pro of an informal assignment is that it may avoid unnecessary internal fighting. Each organization may tackle the issue idiosyncratically. When the Briefer is a strong, trusted advisor to the CEO, that may be a moot point as few will question a more formal designation. Just remember the quote below: "Options can come from anywhere… The critical piece is the understanding of the whole picture, and that is what you need intelligence for." [*Unnamed 3-Star General*]

Quick takeaways for the road:

Incentives for "window dressing" are way more powerful than incentives for open flow of information.

Strategic intelligence is never about accuracy; Placing market developments in context allows better judgement calls, not a crystal ball.

"I needed a conceptual understanding. The problem was that people are focused on the day-to-day events... We break things down to understand the pieces but do a bad job of integrating them back up... We need to be able to rearrange things differently, to get different perspectives, and we need to provide incentives to do this, to reward people for this."

"Intelligence is really important because it is related to decisions that the commander has to make. What is the enemy doing? What are our own forces doing? What are my options? That is what intelligence is for; it is to understand how options can be pursued. We don't think like that unfortunately. We are not connecting stratgetic intelligence with decisions and operations."

"...there are three types of people: those who create options; those who sustain options; and those who give away options."

"Options can come from anywhere... The critical piece is the understanding of the whole picture, and that is what you need intelligence for." Unnamed 3-Star General

Chapter 19:
The Intelligence Revolution and *You*

Opportunity intelligence is new. Opportunity intelligence has always been there.

Contradiction? Not really. People have realized moments of strategic market insights throughout history. What is changing is the amount of noise obscuring these insights. The need to filter the noise to enable growth has never been greater.

The analogy with the emerging space of Revenue Intelligence discussed with the Gong platform adds urgency to the new area of Opportunity Intelligence. For the first time, a piece of software captures and digitalizes the entire exchange between salespeople and customers and then distills it into opportunities for more sales in a feedback loop. The ability to measure the effect directly and quickly may be the one datum changing management's perspective about the much larger space of strategic (competitive) intelligence.

That is if executives focus on raising revenues through market insights. Some do not. It is easier to increase short-term profit by slashing costs. If the organization is bloated, that's just common sense. But it is also lazy work. Increasing revenue is way more challenging. Executives who succeed in that are handsomely rewarded.

This book makes an unequivocal claim that intelligence about potential opportunities for a competitive edge comes from the entire organization. Shutting off channels for opportunity intelligence in a typical corporate bureaucratic hierarchy is a sure way to lose your way.

Competitive doesn't mean benchmarking

I never thought I'd be a competitive intelligence analyst. Thirty years as an analyst, an educator, a trainer, and a mentor in competitive intelligence taught me that the attraction of the elusive hunt for insight is based on dissatisfaction with merely carrying on busy work. But how do you move managers, inundated with routine work and long hours, to make room for an uncertain quest with no clear reward at the end? Sticking one's neck out and pronouncing "I strongly believe there is an opportunity here" can be scary.

In training market-facing managers-- engineers, scientists, business development, researchers, planners, and more-- to derive market insights from mere data, the first question I ask them sounds silly: How do you define "competitive"?

The reason to start at this basic concept is that too many managers believe "competitive intelligence" is search hacks on Google. One doesn't get to be a world-class opportunity analyst on search hacks. One just gets to be a hack.

When we go back-and-forth with hundreds of managers, the discussion typically ends up here: "Anything that gives you an advantage over others *competing* for your company's customers."

An advantage in any market can be cost and/or willingness to pay (a famous Porter-Rivkin economic framework[37]). Either way, a customer prefers your company's *value proposition* to others. Not surprisingly, this applies to internal competition for management attention as well.

Once the meaning of "competitive" is widely shared and agreed upon, the next step in making managers comfortable with the "hunt" is: Can we derive the *entire* meaning of competitive intelligence just from that one word, *competitive?*

My answer is a resounding Yes, but there are other perspectives. Over the years, proliferation (or segmentation) of definitions of competitive intelligence into such terms as marketing, market, competitor, competitive, business, or strategic intelligence made a clear-cut shared understanding difficult. Therefore, the first necessary step for you, the reader, to develop a sense of market insight is to have a simple yet powerful account of the term competitive intelligence. Such understanding sets up the quick subconscious scanning of the environment to flag potential incongruities. Incongruities lead to a deliberate flashing out of insights which leads to imagining possible moves/countermoves.

An unprecedented amount of external information in various areas collected by multiple managers and departments bombards large corporations today. This information is siloed, compartmentalized, disjointed, and often redundant, but it doesn't matter if they call it intelligence or clam chowder. The only thing that matters is a deep sense among employees that competitive advantage drives growth and growth drive job security, promotions, and recognition. Temporary or sustainable, local or global - advantage is at the heart of competition, and competitive intelligence is at the heart of competitive advantage.

If your clam chowder could bring you a competitive advantage, then it is competitive intelligence. It's that simple.

The advantage always depends on third parties

George Orwell famously said, "We have now sunk to the depth at which restatement of the obvious is the first duty of an intelligent man." A competitive edge exists only as long as high-impact players out there haven't yet discovered it, haven't made the first move on it, and/or will not respond in such a way as to nullify it once a company makes a move. So, following Orwell's lament, here is sinking to the depth of the obvious: Other players affect your company's continuous attempt to create an edge.

To confound growth even further, the concept of "advantage" is never independent of actors' assumptions and cognitive schemas. Some will take advantage of the fact that opportunities are subjective, depend on premises, and are always speculative. People who don't know an opportunity from their elbow will typically cover it up with buzz words using terms such as "synergy" and "disruption."[38] Buzz words use the audience's cognitive schema to "sell" service or a business deal, but it doesn't necessarily reflect real opportunity (or real risk). Disruptions are few and far between; competition is not. Synergy often is an empty slogan; real premiums paid for acquisitions that reflect late discovery of potential in the market are not.

Those who pigeonhole competitive intelligence as the formal activity of "collecting competitor/market information, analyzing it and disseminating it" as if this exercise yields competitive advantage by magic are also those who say competitive strategy is whatever results from a strategy development process.

That's just busywork, and it has little to do with intelligence or competitive strategy.

The most important question of all - what does it take to create competitive advantage - is at the heart of the art of strategy and the skill of deriving strategic market insight. Corporate functionaries who need to categorize/confine insight activities to a specific department might find the concept slippery.

Who and what to ignore when it comes to encouraging employees' perspectives on strategic market insights?

Several chapters in this book focused on organizational obstacles to finding opportunities. Personal doubts play an important role as well. Managers may be discouraged from expressing their perspective on market insights by common myths about what is and what isn't competitive intelligence. Here are two such common hurdles the reader should actively learn to ignore.

1. You don't need to hunt alone

   Opportunities are speculations about the future. Many managers aren't confident that they know enough about the business to spot a strategic opportunity. Who says that their market insight is correct?

   There is no need to hunt alone for insight. Instead, gather a few colleagues whose skills you respect and make it a group project. Share the framework with them. Explain your reasoning. Let them play competitors and customers and regulators' reactions.

2. Don't let the "actionable" mantra stop you.

The most common misunderstanding is that intelligence must be actionable information. What if management didn't act because of broader considerations? What if an executive (I met a few) believes he doesn't need any competitive insight because he has a "formula" for success that "never" fails? What if the information actually called for not acting[39]? If Jeff Immelt, GE's former CEO, listened to the voices inside GE that warned about the acquisition of troublesome Alstom, GE would have been much better off today, and he might have still been the CEO.

My recommendation: Ignore this definition that equates intelligence with action. It is sexy, it is consistent with the desire to *do something*, but it is short-sighted.

The burden on the manager or analyst to make management act, rather than make management *recognize an insight* it didn't think about before (part and parcel of "sensemaking"), is misguided. Advantage is never objective, openly available, and detached from the user's own agenda, beliefs, and blinders. Therefore, the test is not "actionable recommendations" so popular with consultants and yet often completely ignored by the top users who fail to see the reality of the action or at what cost the impact. The real test is the effect on the user's perspective. The manager/analyst is the filter of the background noise. Taking their insight into a plan of action (strategy options) and showing its potential impact on the bottom line takes time and effort. The first step is an initial nod by management, who comes to see the opportunity *it didn't see before.*

3. Get around operational cowboys

Another myth is that the planning and intelligence *process* is more important than the insight itself. The worshippers of "processes" have led not one company into decline. Those who buy into the mythology of "strong culture and good team" as sufficient for success and strategy as just a sideshow are often (not always!) operational guys who never actually created a strategy of their own, just executed someone else's. There is a reason why managing is not the same as leading. Operational managers tasked with ensuring smooth and efficient operations under a given strategy may not be the best route to introducing new strategic thinking. Their attention is on better, faster, and more efficient executing the *current operations*, and rightly so. Don't get discouraged if a VP Technology says this is not what we should be thinking about, or a CFO discounts potential impact because the numbers are not there yet.

Is it a learned skill?

Learning to think about competition and advantages can be intuitive. Startup entrepreneurs do it all the time, as do small business owners like the one who owns your neighborhood hardware store. However, it is not so intuitively easy in a large company with multiple product lines, global markets, and a broad spectrum of possible surprises. Instead, it's a skill based on a schema of market forces and, at times, the ability to see through the implicit assumptions of users.

Job descriptions for competitive intelligence reflect management mischaracterizing how insights are derived and confining the search for it to a specific function.[40] Opportunity Intelligence is not a dedicated position. It's an alert mindset of seeing options for growth in a complex world of noise and the very subjective realm of (at times utterly blind) users. No recruiter puts *that* into a job description.

Opportunity Intelligence is *your* future

The above makes the alertness to potential insights meshing with top management's search for growth more critical but also so much more difficult because it is plainly not generic research on steroids.

The true insight is even more profound: If searching for opportunities is not defined as a specific role but as information that materially affects management thinking about competitive advantage, it turns close interactions with those in power crucial. Moreover, seeing *early* signs of shifts in the market is, by definition, based on less data than required for the Big Data paradigm, and by default, involves a nonlinear perspective. Linear perspective assumes things progress linearly. Linear managers wait until a secondary source- a news source- reports on the early phenomenon. By the time a reporter notices a market shift, the opportunity is gone.

Competitive convergence

While waiting for more data is reasonable for operational decisions, strategic insights are rare, capturing glimpses of an unfolding future that is at best, uncertain, or at worst, ambiguous. As a result, it is much safer to stick to an existing strategy, execute tactical initiatives, and remain in the game. In competitive convergence, most large players benchmark each other and follow similar moves. What growth-oriented executives need, though, is someone to tell them, Oh our exalted leaders, what we see from here might be priceless if you just listen.

Case in Point

Competitive convergence is way more prevalent than people realize. Under continuous pressure by Wall Street for short-term profits, the race to operational efficiencies far outweighs the search for new growth opportunities. The press falls quickly in step, blurring the line between efficiency and distinction. Nowhere is the case more evident than in the Airline industry.

Recent capital spending by both Delta and United represents one such example when contrasted with Southwest Airlines. The press highlighted these airlines' different fleet-mix purchase decisions as a massive bet on the strategic difference[40]. Delta is adding capacity by retiring smaller aircraft, replacing them with narrow-body regional jets with more seats, and closing two small hubs. United adding capacity through a different mix of larger aircraft and does not close hubs. A different perspective will see this as not so much a strategic difference but an operational difference as the never-ending race to efficiency (higher capacity, lower cost per seat) continues.

In contrast, Southwest Airlines has been operating on a distinctly different strategy for decades, cementing its dominance over domestic air traffic. Passengers preferred its no-frill, short point-to-point, frequent flights over legacy airlines' dependency on connections in congested Hubs. In 2021, moreover, Delta and United Airlines' expansion strategy evidently depends on an assumption of massive market expansion without a moment of hesitation to reckon with each other's similarly optimistic perspective. The more likely outcome of the casual attention to other players' moves will be overcapacity, fare wars, low margins, forced cut downs on capacity later, almost inevitable debt and management "restructuring" in the future. Give it three years?

Delta and United are not the exceptions. Management attention divides roughly into 99% operational/cost/efficiencies issues and 1% new opportunities. Leadership's attention should be the reverse. This is one clear difference between managing and leading. Unfortunately, the popular business press hardly addresses that.

A company needs a big boss who is open to the idea that *someone else* in the organization can think competitively (aside from his investment banker's pal). These wise words of the 3-Star General should be a warning and a revelation: "The issue is how to be both a consumer of intelligence and a driver of intelligence. Assuming you have inquisitive commanders, it's not about problem-solving. It's about co-producing and co-consuming."

Now go out and conquer the world. You know from where the advantage springs.

Quick takeaways for the road:

You don't get to be a world-class opportunity analyst on search hacks. You just get to be a hack.

Intelligence is not synonymous with actionable information despite it being a popular definition. The real test is its effect on perspective. Action might follow.

"The issue is how to be both a consumer of intelligence and a driver of intelligence. Assuming you have inquistive commanders, it's not about problem solving. It's about co-producting and co-consuming." Unnamed 3-Star General

Epilogue

THERE WILL BE
HELL TO PAY
BENJAMIN GILAD

What is an insight?

In the business world, one hears the term insight thrown around freely. Intelligence and strategic market insights are hardly distinguishable from each other. But cheapening the word via labeling every trivial statement an "insight" prevents companies and leaders from benefitting from *true* insight, as defined below.

The best definition I ever heard was from Stan Sthanunathan, formerly the Executive Vice President of Consumer and Market Insights at Unilever, who defines insight as a "'oh s&!t' moment." It's when a decision-maker says, "oh my g*d, I never thought of it that way." Insight, by definition, is something not obvious. It is, by default, a counter-intuitive perspective. Unexpected, un-thought about previously, unconventional, outside the consensus. It is often counter-cultural, early, not easily fitting into an existing schema. However, the term "think out of the box" doesn't capture the true essence of insight because insight can pop up *in the box.*

Insight is not the result of deliberate, systematic effort. It is arrived at as a burst of creative/imaginative thinking changing one's previously held beliefs, assumptions, and perspective. It is the result of alertness to opportunities, a System 1's subconscious hunt.

The central insight of this book is simple but far from trivial:

Executives who fail to tap their own people for opportunity intelligence are missing out big time on a resource close at hand.

Corollary 1: Executives who believe they already thought through all growth options are leaving a lot of money on the table.

Corollary 2: Money left on a table will be taken away by someone else.

Corollary 3: One doesn't need expensive IT to tap into employee's alertness to opportunities. All one needs is to open a safe bypass channel.

Corollary 4: Training market-facing teams in the skill underlying market insight - recognizing early signs of change- may have the highest ROI of any investment a company makes in organizational development.

Corollary 5: If you needed this book to change your perspective on competitive intelligence, this was an insight. If you didn't need it, it wasn't an insight for you, but it might be for others. Please share it. Alternatively, if you prefer to rely on luck, there will be hell to pay if it's not enough[42].

End Notes

CHAPTER 1

1   https://productcraft.com/perspectives/tactical-vs-strategic-where-product-managers-really-spent-their-time-in-2019/

2   https://www.sfgnetwork.com/blog/data-services/the-importance-of-real-time-data/

CHAPTER 2

3   https://www.brightline.org/resources/eiu-report/

4   From P&W website: "The PT6A engine family is the world's most popular engine in its class and is one of Pratt & Whitney's greatest success stories. Experience gained from the PT6A has helped spawn many of the engine families that have made Pratt & Whitney a world leader in the gas turbine engine market." From Forbes: "It will be nearly impossible for a competitor to keep up without introducing its own version of a geared system, and at this point Pratt & Whitney presumably holds most of the key patents." https://www.forbes.com/sites/lorenthompson/2020/12/02/pratt--whitneys-geared-turbofan-is-poised-to-emerge-from-the-pandemic-in-great-shape/?sh=1f15a7071655

CHAPTER 3

5   https://www.greenbook.org/mr/getting-it-right/achieving-insights-success-at-unilever/

6   Michael Porter: *Competitive Strategy*. (Free Press, 1980, 1999).

7   This section is based on M.E Porter, Competitive Strategy. Free Press, 1980 and 1999.

8   https://knowledge.wharton.upenn.edu/article/anatomy-of-a-merger-hostile-deals-become-friendly-in-the-end-right/

CHAPTER 4

9   More on these two distinct cognitive processes, see Daniel Kahneman, *Thinking- Fast and Slow*. Penguin, 2011.

10   The concept of alertness to opportunities was first coined by Israel Kirzner. See his seminal work Perception, Opportunity and Profit. University of Chicago Press, 1979.

11   https://www.cato.org/policy-report/march/april-2021/how-i-became-libertarian

12   https://www.inc.com/jason-aten/this-was-steve-jobs-most-important-observation-when-he-returned-to-apple-it-changed-everything.html

13   https://eyeonhousing.org/2020/09/how-many-homes-are-concrete-framed/

14   https://www.msn.com/en-us/news/us/weyerhaeuser-ceo-devin-stockfish-on-the-housing-boom-inflation-and-monetizing-forests-in-the-battle-against-climate-change/ar-AALjAMX?ocid=msedgdhp

CHAPTER 7

15   https://www.merriam-webster.com/words-at-play/deduction-vs-induction-vs-abduction

16   https://www.vox.com/recode/2019/7/3/18716431/walmart-jet-marc-lore-modcloth-amazon-ecommerce-losses-online-sales

17   https://nypost.com/2020/05/19/walmart-shutting-down-jet-com-after-buying-it-four-years-go-for-3-3b/

18   https://www.cbinsights.com/research/biggest-startup-failures/

19   https://www.usatoday.com/story/entertainment/tv/2020/10/22/quibi-shuts-down-after-six-months-heres-why/3725358001/

CHAPTER 10

20   https://business.linkedin.com/content/dam/me/business/en-us/marketing-solutions/resources/pdfs/the-objectivity-trap-spreads-v2.pdf

21   ibid

CHAPTER 11

22   For some anecdotal evidence see: https://gigaom.com/2011/02/23/why-most-startup-acquisitions-fail-and-always-will/ and https://www.inc.com/steve-blank/why-corporate-acquisitions-of-startups-fail.html

23   https://paygo.media/p/25171

24   https://www.cnbc.com/2020/02/19/its-never-been-this-hard-for-companies-to-find-qualified-workers.html

CHAPTER 12

25   Can it be related to divergent thinking? Test yours here: https://www.datcreativity.com/

CHAPTER 14

26   https://www.msn.com/en-us/news/us/texas-power-grid-run-by-ercot-set-up-the-state-for-disaster/ar-BB1dSg2O?ocid=msedgdhp

CHAPTER 15

27   https://www.greenbook.org/mr/getting-it-right/achieving-insights-success-at-unilever/

CHAPTER 16

28   Fear of Missing Out, Fear of Messing Up.

29   *Noise: A Flaw in Human Judgment* by Daniel Kahneman, Olivier Sibony and Cass R. Sunstein (Little, Brown and Company, 2021)

30   See https://www.geektime.com/israeli-startup-gong-raises-250m-at-7-25b-valuation/ and https://siliconangle.com/2021/06/03/revenue-intelligence-startup-gong-raises-250m-series-e-funding/

31   B. Gilad and T. Gilad, *The Business Intelligence System.* AMACOM, 1988.

CHAPTER 17

32   Academy of Competitive Intelligence, 2019. Accessible via https://academyci.com/how-ci-changed-in-one-decade-survey-report/

33   https://nationalpost.com/news/exclusive-did-huawei-bring-down-nortel-corporate-espionage-theft-and-the-parallel-rise-and-fall-of-two-telecom-giants

CHAPTER 18

34   On the failure of analogies in strategic decisions, see Gavetti, Giovanni M., and Jan W. Rivkin. "Use and Abuse of Analogies." Harvard Business School Background Note 703-429, February 2003. (Revised February 2006.)

35   Adrian Wolfberg, "The President's Daily Brief: Managing the Relationship between Intelligence and the Policymaker". Political Science Quarterly, Volume 132 Number 2, 2017, pp. 225-258.

36   Adrian Wolfberg, "When generals consume intelligence: the problems that arise and how they solve them." Intelligence and National Security, 2017 VOL. 32, NO. 4, 460–478

http://dx.doi.org/10.1080/02684527.2016.1268359

CHAPTER 19

37   https://www.hbs.edu/faculty/Pages/item.aspx?num=27306

38   For a brilliant and hilarious article on new age language with little meaning, see https://www.msn.com/en-us/lifestyle/lifestyle-buzz/why-does-everyone-talk-like-they-re-in-a-cult/ar-AAL1Sf9?ocid=msedgdhp&pc=U531

39   My colleague, mark Chussil, of Advanced Competitive Strategies, makes exactly this point in our book, The NEW Employee Manual (Entrepreneur Press, 2019).

40   More on the fictitious element in job descriptions see B. Gilad and M. Chussil, *The NEW Employee Manual- A No Holds Barred Look at Corporate Life.* Entrepreneur Press, 2019.

41   https://www.msn.com/en-us/money/companies/united-airlines-and-delta-air-lines-choose-different-fleet-strategies/ar-AALV1aZ?ocid=msedgdhp&pc=U531

EPILOGUE

42   Benjamin Gilad, *There Will Be Hell To Pay*. Black Rose Writing, 2018.